THE LIFE OF SALADIN

Sir Hamilton Gibb

THE LIFE OF SALADIN

Based on the Works of
Baha' ad-Din ibn Shaddad *and* 'Imad ad-Din al-Isfahani

Foreword by
Robert Irwin

Saqi Essentials

London   San Francisco

ISBN 10: 0-86356-928-5
ISBN 13: 978-0-86356-928-9

First published in 1973 by The Clarendon Press, Oxford University Press
This edition published 2006 by Saqi Books

A full CIP record for this book is available from the British Library
A full CIP record for this book is available from the Library of Congress

Manufactured in Lebanon

SAQI
26 Westbourne Grove, London W2 5RH
825 Page Street, Suite 203, Berkeley, California 94710
www.saqibooks.com

Contents

Foreword

by Robert Irwin

'I saw Saladin, aloof, alone.' In his *Divine Comedy* Dante placed Saladin in Limbo with the virtuous Greek philosophers whose only crime had been that they had not had the opportunity to embrace Christianity. In the Middle Ages Saladin's reputation was at least as established in Christendom as it was in the Islamic lands. William of Tyre, the chronicler of the Crusader Kingdom of Jerusalem, described Saladin as 'a man of acute genius, prompt in arms, and liberal above average'. In Western Europe Saladin became the hero of several romances in which he was credited with French noble birth (through his mother) and was presented as a heroic jouster and model of chivalry.

Saladin (more properly Salah al-Din) was born of Kurdish stock in the region of Tikrit in Iraq. Saladin's father Ayyub and his kinsmen entered the service of Nur al-Din, the Turkish ruler of Aleppo and later Damascus. In 1169 Saladin was part of a mixed force of Turks and Kurds sent by Nur al-Din against the Fatimid Caliph in Egypt. In 1174 Saladin dethroned the last Fatimid and took power in his own right. He continued to pay lip service to Nur al-Din, but after the latter's death in 1181 Saladin occupied Damascus. In the years that followed Saladin waged various campaigns against rival Muslim princes in Syria, Iraq and Yemen. He also launched sporadic invasions of the Kingdom of Jerusalem. These achieved little until in 1187 Saladin led an army across the Jordan and, by commencing a siege of the town of Tiberias, lured Guy de Lusignan on to a waterless march towards military disaster at the Battle of Hattin. In the wake of his victory Saladin was able to occupy Jerusalem and the greater part of the Crusader Kingdom. However, the loss of Jerusalem provoked the preaching of the Third Crusade and the despatch of large English, French and German contingents to the Holy Land. Although Saladin was successful in fighting Richard the Lionheart's Crusader force to a standstill, the struggle emptied the coffers of Egypt and Syria and weakened the Sultan's health. Saladin's Ayyubid siblings and descendants were to rule over Egypt and various provinces of Syria, from the Sultan's death in 1193 until the mid-thirteenth century, when they were deposed by the Turkish Mamluks.

In *The Decline and Fall of the Roman Empire* Edward Gibbon presented Saladin as a Muslim saint:

> Both in faith and practice he was a rigid Musulman: he ever deplored that the defence of religion had not allowed him to accomplish the pilgrimage of Mecca, but at the stated hours, five times each day, the sultan devoutly prayed with his brethren: the involuntary omission of fasting was scrupulously repaid; and his perusal of the Koran, on horseback between the approaching armies, may be quoted as a proof, however ostentatious, of piety and courage.

Sir Walter Scott made Saladin one of the heroes of *The Talisman* (1825), a novel that Hamilton Gibb used to recommend to his students as 'a work of art from which they could learn much about Islamic history'. Thomas Carlyle (1795–1881) did not, I think, write about Saladin, though he did write an influential life of Muhammad and he was certainly read by all the leading British Orientalists of the nineteenth century. In *Heroes and Hero-Worship* (1841) Carlyle presented history as being primarily the story of heroes, great men who rose above the common crowd to offer that crowd hope, and whose examples should inspire emulation. More generally, the Carlylean way of recreating the past offered a romantic vision in which 'only Poetry is History'. Those who followed in Carlyle's footsteps stressed narrative and vividly imagined scenes, dramatic moments. History was 'the essence of innumerable biographies'. It is clear that Carlyle's vision of history played a large part in shaping the later lives of Saladin by Carlyle's fellow Scotsmen, Stanley Lane-Poole and Hamilton Gibb.

At the very end of the nineteenth century, thanks to Lane-Poole, Saladin moved from being just a paladin of Islamic chivalry to being one of the heroes of the nations — like William Tell or Garibaldi — though it was never clear from Lane-Poole's narrative of which nation Saladin was a hero. Stanley Lane Poole (1854–1931) was Professor of Arabic at Trinity College Dublin and grandnephew of E.W. Lane. His *Saladin and the Fall of the Kingdom of Jerusalem*, published in the 'Heroes of the Nations' series in London in 1898, presented a hero whose nobility of spirit raised him above his Muslim subjects. Lane-Poole actually felt that the Orientals were incapable of appreciating Saladin's true heroism, concluding his book with these words:

... the character of the great Sultan, however, appeals

more strongly to Europeans than to Moslems, who admire his chivalry less than his warlike triumphs. To us it is the generosity of the character, rather than the success of the career, that makes Saladin a true as well as a romantic hero.

The gentle and scholarly Lane-Poole had presented Saladin as a man in his own image. The same year that Lane-Poole's book was published Kaiser Wilhelm II of Germany made a tour of the Middle East, laying a flag and a wreath dedicated to 'the hero Sultan Saladin' on the Sultan's tomb within the precinct of the Great Mosque in Damascus. Afterwards, the Kaiser made a speech praising him as 'a knight without fear or blame, who often had to teach his opponents the right way to practise chivalry'. He later contributed a further wreath to Saladin's tomb, this time bronze gilt and bearing the vainglorious legend 'From one great emperor to another'.

Sir Hamilton Alexander Rosskeen Gibb (1895–1971) was born in Alexandria. (His father worked for a land reclamation company on the Nile Delta.) From 1900 onwards Hamilton Gibb was educated in Edinburgh at the Royal High School, where Walter Scott attended. Subsequently Gibb began studying Arabic, Hebrew and Aramaic at the city's university, but his studies were interrupted by the First World War, in which he was to see service in France and Italy. After the war he studied at the School of Oriental Studies (which later became the School of Oriental and African Studies) of the University of London. He studied Arabic with the great Islamicist, Sir Thomas Arnold. Awarded an MA in 1922, Gibb went on to teach Arabic at SOAS as lecturer, reader and professor successively (the last after Arnold's retirement in 1930). Sir Cyril Philips, the director of SOAS from 1957–

1976, described Gibb as 'the foremost European Arabist of the day'. In 1937 he moved to Oxford where he succeeded David Margoliouth as Laudian Professor of Arabic.

Gibb was knighted in 1954. In 1955 he went to Harvard as a professor and director of Harvard's Centre for Middle Eastern Studies. His move across the Atlantic was motivated in large part by his conviction that Orientalists needed to break out of their philological strait-jackets and establish closer links with other departments, particularly the social sciences, and he believed Harvard would be more accommodating than Oxford had been. In 1964 he suffered a severe stroke and thereafter, back in Oxford, restricted his research to a few cherished projects. He was preparing to send *The Life of Saladin* to his publishers when he died in 1972.

Gibb wrote on a bewilderingly wide range of topics. Albert Hourani described him as the 'last of the universal Arabists'. Gibb's first major publication *The Arab Conquests in Central Asia* (1923) was based on his research thesis. Other books included *Arabic Literature* (1926), *Modern Trends in Islam* (1947) and *Mohammedanism: An Historical Survey* (1949). Together with the Turkish scholar, Harold Bowen, he produced a two-volume study of the Ottoman Empire, *Islamic Society and the West* (1950 and 1957). He also translated parts of Ibn Qalanisi's history, under the title *The Damascus Chronicle of the Crusades* (1932), and he worked on an unfinished translation of the fourteenth-century travel narrative of Ibn Battuta. (Three volumes appeared in 1956, 1962 and 1971.) Gibb also wrote essays on modern Arabic literature (he was perhaps the first European scholar to do so). Among other short pieces his essay 'An Interpretation of Islamic History', originally published in *The Journal of World History* in 1953, exercised an enormous influence on later historians of the Islamic world. Furthermore, the argument outlined in that essay is essential for understanding Gibb's thinking about the career of Saladin.

Ever since his boyhood immersion in *The Talisman* Saladin had been Gibb's hero and, in addition to *The Life of Saladin*, Gibb produced some important articles: 'The Armies of Saladin' in 'Cahiers de l'Histoire Égyptienne' series 3, no.4 (1951), pp.304–320; 'The Achievement of Saladin' in *Bulletin of the John Rylands Library*, 35 (1952), pp.44–60; 'Al-Barq al-Shami: the History of Saladin by the Katib 'Imad al-Din al-Isfahani' in *Wiener Zeitschrift für die Kunde des Morgenlandes*, 52 (1953), pp.93–115; and 'The Arab Sources for the Life of Saladin' in *Speculum*, (1960), pp. 58–72.

Without directly challenging Lane-Poole's overall interpretation, Gibb put the study of the career of Saladin on a more scientific basis. Gibb, who saw himself primarily as an historian, believed that Islam and the way it evolved over the centuries was central to the history of the Middle East. Throughout his intellectual career he was much influenced by the fourteenth-century philosopher-historian Ibn Khaldun's *Muqaddima* (*Prolegomena*). Ibn Khaldun had argued that Saladin was an exceptional figure who had used the *jihad* to revive the *'isaba*, or social solidarity, of the Muslim community. More generally, Ibn Khaldun searched for the broad social and political forces that lay behind the rise and fall of successive Muslim regimes. This was Gibb's goal also and, according to Anne Lambton, a student of his who went on to become Professor of Persian at SOAS, history for Gibb was 'the search for patterns on the web of human life'. His interpretation of the career of Saladin should be understood within the context of his much grander vision of Islam's past which he had advanced in 'An Interpretation of Islamic

History' in which, in the words of another of his students, Albert Hourani, Gibb 'traced the march of the *umma* (the Muslim community) through the wilderness of religious fantasies, human passions, political conflict, opportunism, and cynicism; or, to be more precise the Sunni *umma* ...' In Gibb's reading of Ibn Khaldun, the principles of the *Shariʿa* (Islamic law) lay behind Ibn Khaldun's exposition of the laws of historical change. The *Shariʿa* played a similarly pivotal role in Gibb's reading of the ideals and goals of Saladin.

Gibb made this vision of Saladin's place in his version of history explicit in his essay 'The Achievement of Saladin'. The just ruler Saladin was pre-eminently a leader who kept the *umma* on the right path, reformed its institutions and rescued it from demoralisation. Whereas Saladin's precursor, Nur al-Din, had 'operated from within the structure of politics of his age', Saladin rose above that structure. He faced down opposition from Shi'is, extremist Sufis and cynics, as well as, of course, Christian Crusaders. But not even Saladin was able to lead his people back to the conditions that prevailed in the heyday of the Abbasid Caliphate of the eighth and ninth centuries when Muslims were more united, more confident and more adventurous in their intellectual investigations. Saladin's prosecution of the *jihad* and his defeat of the Crusaders, though celebrated by medieval and modern historians, was only part of his grander project, Gibb argued: he wanted to put an end to the Muslim political weakness and division that had made the Crusades possible in the first place, and then to spearhead a more general moral rearmament that would unite Muslims spiritually and politically under the Abbasid Caliph in Baghdad. This he did not succeed in doing. So, within this context, Saladin was indeed a hero; but he was also a heroic failure. Things were to fall apart under his quarrelling

Ayyubid kinsmen, and in the thirteenth century there were further Crusades.

In 'The Achievement of Saladin' Gibb wrote as follows:

> Neither warrior nor governor by training or inclination, he it was who inspired and gathered round himself all the elements and forces making for the unity of Islam against the invaders. And this he did, not so much by the example of his personal courage and resolution – which were undeniable – as by his unselfishness, his humility and generosity, his moral vindication of Islam against both its enemies and its professed adherents. He was no simpleton, but for all that an utterly simple and transparently honest man. He baffled his enemies, internal and external, because they expected to find him animated by the same motives as they were, and playing the political game as they played it. Guileless himself, he never expected and seldom understood guile in others – a weakness of which his own family and others took advantage, but only (as a general rule) to come up at the end against his single-minded devotion, which nobody and nothing could bend, to the service of his ideals.

It is an idealistic portrait but one that Gibb believed was clearly warranted by the evidence provided by contemporary sources, particularly those of 'Imad al-Din al-Isfahani and Baha' al-Din Ibn Shaddad.

The Life of Saladin takes a more fact-driven and less visionary approach than the essay 'The Achievement of Saladin', yet the vision is still there and it underpins the political and military narrative. This short book is based on the chapters that Gibb originally wrote for *The Pennsylvania*

History of the Crusades (later *The Wisconsin History of the Crusades*, 6 volumes, 1955–89). For reasons outlined above this is not a triumphalist biography, for Saladin 'fought for his ideals, and fought, not victoriously, but in a measure that fell short of his hopes and ambitions'. In this short monograph Gibb returns again and again to certain key themes: that Saladin was surrounded by cynics and doubters; that he was determined to restore the rule of the *Shari'a* (the religious law); and the enormous difficulty he had in keeping armies in the field for the prolonged campaigns necessary to resist the Crusader armies.

In his narrative Gibb had mainly relied on two contemporary Arabic sources, both of them written by men close to Saladin. The first of the authors, 'Imad al-Din al-Isfahani (1125–1201), was, as his name suggests, born in Isfahan, but migrated westwards to study in Baghdad before serving Nur al-Din and later Saladin as a secretary. As an author he produced *Kharidat al-'Asr*, a great anthology of twelfth-century poets, *Faht al-Qassi*, an account of Saladin's conquest of Jerusalem, and *Barq al-Shami*, a life of Saladin, only part of which has survived. His elaborately mannered and verbose style is hard going. The second source, Baha al-Din Yusuf Ibn Shaddad (1145–1234), was a religious scholar who as Qadi to the army was in Saladin's retinue of administrators, scribes and scholars. Ibn Shaddad wrote *al-Nawadir al-sultaniyya fi al-mahasin al-Yusufiyya*, which is an account of the excellent qualities of Saladin, followed by a more conventional chronicle of Saladin's career to which Baha al-Din added many personal reminiscences. This work has been translated by D.S. Richards as *The Rare and Excellent History of Saladin* (Aldershot, Hants., 2001). There are three other important writers that Gibb knew of but made less use of. Al-Qadi al-Fadil (1135–1200) served Saladin as the head of his chancery from 1171 and acted as his chief adviser. He kept an official diary, only parts of which have survived. He also drafted Saladin's proclamations and official correspondence. He was an elaborately florid writer and his high style was much imitated by later chancery officials and court chroniclers. Ibn Abi Tayyi (1232), a Shi'ite in Aleppo, wrote a chronicle that has only survived in fragments quoted in a later chronicle by Abu Shama and which, as Gibb observed, is more favourable to Saladin (who, of course, was a Sunni) than one would have expected. Finally 'Izz al-Din Ibn al-Athir (1160–1233) wrote a chronicle, *al-Kamil al-tawarikh*, that ran from the Creation to 1231. Ibn al-Athir spent much of his time in Mosul and his account of Saladin reflected the resentment of the Zengid dynasty and its loyalists at the way Saladin had taken over in Damascus after the death of Nur al-Din. Even so, Ibn al-Athir was by no means totally hostile to Saladin, but his admiration was grudging.

Gibb had come down rather hard on the Mosuli chronicler, Ibn al-Athir, to whom he ascribed malicious, propagandist aims. The way then was open for Andrew Ehrenkreutz, in *Saladin* (New York, 1972) to draw on Ibn al-Athir in order to put together a directly contrary view of Saladin as a rapacious warlord who used *jihad* to advance the fortunes of himself and his clan mostly at the expense of his Muslim neighbours. This was done by shifting the focus from Saladin's last years and the rather flukey victory at Hattin to the earlier years when Saladin's main target seemed to be other Muslim princes in Syria rather than the Crusaders. However, Ehrenkreutz's book was so carping and consistently hostile to one of world history's great heroes that it got rough treatment when it appeared. One expert reviewer wrote as follows:

One approaches Ehrenkreutz's work with ready sympathy, hoping for a satisfactory re-examination of Saladin's career, because, seductive though it may be, Gibb's view seems just too good to be true. There are, however, such a number of inaccuracies, major and minor mistakes, slanted or unsupportable interpretations of texts, that one's sympathy evaporates and one begins to feel that perhaps Gibb's Saladin is a more acceptable figure after all. (Donald Richards, 'The Early History of Saladin', *Islamic Quarterly*, 17, 1973, p.158–9)

A more balanced assessment came from Hannes Möhring, who, in *Saladin und die dritte Kreuzzug* (Wiesbaden, 1980), presented the sultan as a conventional leader who conformed to the expectations of his followers. His 'alleged generosity was at times nothing more than a cunning (sometimes even a compulsory) move in the political chess game'. Möhring also drew attention to the eschatological elements that feature in the adulatory writings about Saladin's conquest of Jerusalem and his other achievements. Two years later Malcolm Cameron Lyons and D.E.P. Jackson published *Saladin: The Politics of Holy War*. This book had the great merit of bringing into play underused sources, like the difficult-to-translate letters of Qadi al-Fadil and the poets of the time, including al-Wahrani and Ibn al-'Unayn. Like Gibb, and unlike Ehrenkreutz, their narrative concentrated on Saladin's prosecution of the *jihad* in the last years of his life. They (and Möhring) also paid close attention to Saladin's correspondence with the Abbasid Caliph in Baghdad. Gibb's advocacy of the perfections of Saladin may have led him to underestimate the sincerity and achievements of the Zengid predecessors of Saladin. A more positive picture of those predecessors was presented by

Nikita Elisséeff in *Nur al-Din: un grand prince musulman au temps des croisades* (Damascus, 1967). However, despite all the work that has been done on the life and times of Saladin since Gibb's death, the latter's portrait of the Sultan remains essentially unchallenged – a compact, coherent and intensely sympathetic reconstruction of one of the heroes of Islam.

Preface

THIS narrative of Saladin, based on 'Imad ad-Din and Baha' ad-Din, is intended to present a short account of his life and activities as they are reported by the two historians who were closely associated with him. In opposition to them was the famous Ibn al-Athir, who presents a narrative which is based on the work of 'Imad ad-Din, but deliberately takes the opposite view, as will be shown in the text and footnotes that follow. This narrative simply traces the stages of Saladin's life, and excludes all fiscal and administrative policies. It follows the main features of the Pennsylvania *History of the Crusades,* in the chapter entitled 'Saladin'.

THE life and achievements of Saladin constitute one of the great moments in the history of the Crusades. In literature he appears most frequently as a conquering hero, who fought his enemies victoriously and in the end beat them to a standstill. But closer examination of his actual life reveals him not only as a conqueror, but as a man who struggled with enemies of his own side who finally joined him and fought along with him under his sole command. From this angle we see him as a man who fought for his ideals, and fought, not victoriously, but in a measure that fell short of his hopes and ambitions.

The major historical work written by the most famous writer of his own period was the *al-Kamil fi al-Tarikh* of Ibn al-Athir. His chronicle is the universal source of later historians, and includes an account of the campaigns of Saladin. But unfortunately he wrote a panegyric (rather than a history) of the Zangid princes of Mosul, who were the chief opponents of Saladin. In writing this account he used the *al-Barq al-Shami* of the historian the Katib 'Imad ad-Din al-Isfahani, and, in using it almost throughout the narrative, he rewrites it in his own particular style. The malicious twist, the perversions and propagandist ascriptions that he introduces in many of the passages about Saladin, are all valuable in showing, in a pronounced form, the moral problem with which Saladin was confronted and the cynical attitude towards public life held by the Muslim community.[1]

Almost the only source that records the early life of Saladin is the chronicle of Ibn Abi Tayyi'. He was a Shi'ite of Aleppo, and was hostile to Nur ad-Din but unexpectedly friendly to Saladin. All his works are lost except for quotations cited by later authors.[2]

In view of the peculiarities of Ibn Abi Tayyi' and of Ibn al-Athir as chroniclers, it is obvious that neither of them can be relied upon to solve questions of personality and of motive. If indeed we had nothing else to go by, we should have no means at all of discovering the real quality of Saladin's achievement.

From 1188 the other historian from Mosul, Baha' ad-Din Ibn Shaddad (1145–1234), Saladin's judge of the army, was his confidant. In his account of Saladin, written in a simple and straightforward style, he presents Saladin to us as no ordinary chronicle can, as an intimate friend, dealing with him man to man.[3] Baha' ad-Din may perhaps be called uncritical, but he was no deluded hero-worshipper. His admiration was that of an upright and honest man from whom nothing was concealed, and there can be no question of deliberate suppression or deflection of the truth in his narrative of the last five years of Saladin's life. To have one such source for the history of any medieval prince is rare indeed. The portrait it gives us, however,

---

1. For an analysis of the sources and justification of the views here expressed, see H. A. R. Gibb, 'The Arabic Sources for the Life of Saladin', in *Speculum*, January 1960, pp. 58–72.

2. 1160–1235, practically contemporaneous with Ibn al-Athir.

3. Baha' ad-Din Ibn Shaddad (1145–1234). *Al-Nawadir al-sultaniyya*, ed. Schultens, Leyden, 1787, and Cairo, 1317/1899–1900.

is that of Saladin at the height of his success and in the desperate climate of the Third Crusade; it supplies, therefore, little direct reference to the long and hard struggle to build up his power.

In these circumstances, it is a piece of incredible good fortune that our fourth source, which covers (in the original text or in reliable summaries) the whole of his active career, is almost equally close and authoritative. This is the series of professional diaries of Saladin's private secretary, the *katib* (the secretary) 'Imad ad-Din al-Isfahani (1125–1201).[1] Of these volumes two (out of seven) have survived, as well as the separate work covering the campaigns of 1187–93, and fairly copious extracts of the missing years.

'Imad ad-Din belonged to the new class of college-trained civil servants. He entered the employment, first of the Seljuq sultans and of the Caliphate in Iraq, then rose to high rank at Damascus in the service of Nur ad-Din and became secretary to Saladin in 1175. He was one of the most famous stylists of his age and his writings are composed in the elaborate and florid rhyming prose cultivated by the secretarial class. Yet, in such a master of language and vocabulary, the fact that his narratives are cast in this medium does not detract from their clarity and their precision. On closer examination 'Imad ad-Din's statements

---

1. Al-Katib 'Imad ad-Din al-Isfahani (1125-1201). He rose to high rank in the service of the sultans and the Caliphate in Baghdad (where he wrote a work on their administration which was subsequently abridged by al-Bundari) and later of Nur ad-Din and became secretary to Saladin from 1175. In this post he wrote an account of his experience in the service of Saladin, entitled *al-Barq al-Shami*, of which two volumes have survived at Oxford (vol. III, MS. Bruce, 11; vol. V, MS. Marsh, 425), but the greater part of his book has survived in the work of Abu Shama. He subsequently wrote a smaller work on the victories of Saladin and his struggle with the Crusaders, *al-Fath al-Qussi*, ed. Landberg, Leyden, 1886. See my article on *al-Barq ash-Shami* in *Wiener Zeitschrift für die Kunde des Morgenlandes*, LII, 93–115, for the analysis of the two volumes.

are remarkably sober. They are, leaving aside all questions of literary style, not unlike the reports of a conscientious civil servant – as indeed he was. It is almost a paradox that so solid and matter-of-fact a chronicle should be clothed in a garment of such literary exuberance. There is scarcely a sentence, even in the loftiest passages, of direct panegyric of Saladin himself. Certainly 'Imad ad-Din shows a deep admiration for Saladin, but his greatness appears wholly as a corollary from the facts themselves, and only occasionally does he express some criticism of his master.

A further argument for 'Imad ad-Din's accuracy is found in the statements of other first-hand chronicles. Where there are statements of fact by William of Tyre or Ernoul, there is an astonishing degree of identity in general, which often extends even into details.

There is the further question raised by the relation of Abu Shama (1203–67) and his abstract from the original text of the *al-Barq al-Shami*.[1] For on this we have to rely for about two-thirds of the entire book. The answer is a straight one. Abu Shama's abridgment is made with skill and care, leaving out the purely literary elaboration and much of the original and personal quality. Nevertheless, 'Imad ad-Din's narrative is preserved in selection, and what he himself has written is always carefully distinguished.

In addition to the texts that we can use, we have also the *mutajaddidat* (now, alas, only the few citations in later authors that have survived) and the still abundant letters and documents made by al-Qadi al-Fadil, Saladin's faithful *wazir* and friend in

---

1. *The Two Gardens, Kitab al-Rawdatain*, by Abu Shama, summarizing the works of 'Imad ad-Din, Ibn al-Athir, and other writers, e. Cairo, 1287, and vol. I, part 1 by M. Hilmi M. Ahmad, Cairo, 1956.

Egypt. A few have been collected and edited but the majority are still to be found in various manuscript collections. And finally there are casual mentions in other works (for example, the Spanish traveller Ibn Jubair) and the Egyptian land agent, Ibn Mammati, whose book on the lands of Egypt was produced just after Saladin's death,[1] and two chronicles written in the next generation, that of Aleppo by Ibn al-'Adim, and that of Syria, the *Mufarrij al-kurub* by Ibn Wasil (ed. **G**. al-Shayyal, Cairo, 1953–60), both of which repeat many of the perversions of Ibn al-Athir.

Saladin (named Yusuf) spent his childhood in Ba'albak and other castles where his father Ayyub was governor, first as castellan for Zangi and subsequently on behalf of the government of Damascus. At the age of fourteen, in 1152, he joined his uncle Shirkuh in the service of the sultan Nur ad-Din and was alloted a fief.[2] In 1156 he succeeded his elder brother Turanshah as his uncle's deputy in the military governorship of Damascus, but relinquished the post after a short time in protest against the fraudulence of the chief accountant. He then rejoined Nur ad-Din at Aleppo and became one of his close associates, 'never leaving him whether on the march or at court'.[3] Later on he again held the office of deputy commandant at Damascus[4] for an unspecified period. Apart from his skill in polo (inherited from his father) and an interest in religious studies, probably inspired by his admiring emulation of Nur ad-Din, nothing is known of his early years.

---

1. See H. Helbig, *Al-Qadi al-Fadil* for an analysis of a few of his rescripts. The Spanish traveller Ibn Jubair was edited by W. Wright (G.M.S. vol. V, Leiden, 1907), and the work of Ibn Mammati by 'Aziz Suryal 'Atiya (Cairo, 1943).
2. Ibn Abi Tayyi' in Abu Shama, I, 84 = Hilmi Ahmad, I, i, 209-10.
3. Ibn Abi Tayyi' in Abu Shama, I, 100 = Hilmi Ahmad, I, i, 252. For relations of Saladin and Nur ad-Din, see N. Elisséef, *Nur ad-Din*, Damascus, 1967.
4. 'Imad ad-Din in Abu Shama, I, 262.

The first campaigns of Shirkuh, on behalf of Nur ad-Din, were unsuccessful. In 1164 he was besieged by Amalric's crusaders and the Egyptians under Shawar at Bilbays and was fortunate in Nur ad-Din's armistice. In 1167 Shirkuh was again accompanied by Saladin and fought a battle south of Cairo in which Amalric was routed. Then he marched north to Alexandria, where he left Saladin in command, himself returning to Upper Egypt. Saladin held out for seventy-five days, and was eventually relieved by Shirkuh's arrangement to make peace with the Egyptians. Saladin spent some days in the Frankish camp, perhaps as a hostage, and he probably had an opportunity to make a friendship with Humphrey of Toron.

When, for the third time, Shirkuh was ordered into Egypt at the end of 1168, on the urgent entreaty of the Fatimid caliph al-'Adid, Saladin, on his own statement, submitted unwillingly to Nur ad-Din's command to accompany him. 'I felt as if I was going to my death', he said.[1] It seems evident that Nur ad-Din intended the occupation to be a permanent one this time; according to Ibn al-Athir, the Fatimid caliph had, indeed, asked that it should be so, and had made provision for fiefs to be given to the Syrian officers (or rather their mamluks).[2] He gave Shirkuh the command of two thousand of his own guard, the Asadiya, called by the title of Asad ad-Din (the name of Shirkuh) and six thousand of the Turkman troops, paid for by him.

1. The most reliable source is Saladin's own statement to Baha' ad-Din (Schultens, 33 = Cairo, 31). Ibn al-Athir's vivid narrative is related at second-hand from an anonymous source (XI, 226) and is not above suspicion in its details. Nothing bearing on the subject is quoted from 'Imad ad-Din, but Abu Shama (I, 155-6) cites a contemporary poem by the Damascus poet Hassan al-'Arqalah in which, while praising Saladin, he chides him for hanging back from the expedition to Egypt.

2. Ibn al-Athir Kamil al-Tawarikh, ed. Tornberg, Leiden, 1853–64, XI, 222, and cf. 223, 20.

Saladin's first exploit on the advance into Egypt was the seizure of the intriguing *wazir*, Shawar, who had been responsible for calling in the Franks, and his execution on the caliph's orders. Shirkuh was invested with the wazirate and the administration was directed on his behalf by Saladin (this most probably being the reason, indeed, why Nur ad-Din had insisted on his accompanying his uncle to Egypt).[1]

When Shirkuh died suddenly nine weeks later, the amirs proposed Shihab ad-Din Mahmud al-Harimi, Saladin's maternal uncle, as his successor, but he, fearing the opposition of some of them, advised al-'Adid to appoint Saladin. The nomination was made in consequence, although some of Nur ad-Din's officers resented it and returned to Syria.[2] The official diploma of his investiture on 26 March 1169, with the title of al-Malik an-Nasir ('the victorious king'), is still extant. It was composed by his devoted friend and counsellor, the al-Qadi al-Fadil,[3] and amongst its grandiloquent periods there is one prophetic phrase:

---

1. Abu Shama, I, 159, 2–3.

2. Ibn al-Athir's narrative, which represents Saladin as the choice of the Fatimid court in the hope of exploiting his youth and weak military position, is open to serious objections; 'Imad ad-Din, on the contrary (who was at the time private secretary at Damascus and in a position to know the facts), asserts that the amirs, after some disagreement and discussion, agreed on Saladin and 'forced the lord of the palace to appoint him'. Ibn Abi Tayyi' (in Abu Shama, I, 173) mentions Mahmud al-Harimi as the first nominee of the amirs, but owing to the opposition of some of them he advised al-'Adid to appoint Saladin. As for Saladin's military strength, there is no question that he succeeded to the command of Shirkuh's regiment (Asadiya) (cf Ibn Abi Tayyi' in Abu Shama, I, 172) which was probably the strongest unit of Syrians. But the fact of the desertion of some of the Turkish amirs is confirmed not only by their return to Syria, but also by their subsequent hostility to Saladin; see for Ghars ad-Din Qilij, Abu Shama, I, 249, and for Qutb ad-Din Yanal al-Manbiji, Abu Shama, I, 249 and 256, foot, and Ibn al-Athir, XI, 284.

3. The diploma is edited by Helbig, op. cit., pp. 53–61. The passage is on P. 60, and is cited also by Abu Shama, I, 161.

'As for the *jihad*, thou art the nursling of its milk and the child of its bosom. Gird up therefore the shanks of spears to meet it and to plunge on its service into a sea of swordpoints; ... until God give the victory which the Commander of the Faithful hopeth to be laid up for thy days and to be witness for thee when thou shalt stand in His presence'.[1]

The main obstacle, of course, was the Egyptian army, composed of several regiments of white cavalry and some thirty thousand Sudani infantry.[2] Saladin (we are told) immediately began to build up his army at the expense of the Egyptian officers, and when a revolt broke out among the black, he

---

1. Baha' ad-Din's further statement on the change in Saladin's conduct and renunciation of wine, etc. (Schultens, 35 = Cairo, 32–3) from that time is perhaps reminiscent of Ibn Abi Tayyi' (Abu Shama, I, 173). The term *Sultan* occurs in the diploma of investment of Shirkuh, the caliph's superscription being addressed as *Sultan al-juyush*, 'the Sultan of the forces' (Abu Shama, I, 159, 8) and is repeated (with reference to Shirkuh) in that of Saladin (Helbig, op. cit., p. 58, l. 9). This text confirms the statement of Abu Shama (I, 130, l. 13) that in Fatimid Egypt the term *Sultan* was applied to the *wazir* in his capacity as the commander of the Faithful's armies, and that in the person of Saladin this sense merged into the sense of 'temporal sovereign' which had become current in Asia in the Seljuq period. There is no indication that the title of *Sultan* was at any time 'conferred' on Saladin by the 'Abbasid caliph; on the contrary, he continued to be styled officially and on his coinage by the Egyptian vizierial title *al-Malik an-Nasir*. See further G. Wiet, 'Les Inscriptions de Saladin', in *Syria* (1922), pp. 30–28. *For examples of the use of the term* Sultan applied to Saladin before 570/1174, see Ibn Abi Tayyi', *apud* Abu Shama, I, 184, 3 and 6 (6); 192, 15 (566); 196, 18 and 27 (567). The last reference is particularly significant as being a quotation of the official Khutba; 'Imad ad-Din, *apud* Abu Shama, I, 194, 20 and 24 (567), and *Bustan al-Zami'* (ed. Cahen, B.E.O., VII–VIII, 139, 17 (568)).

2. Al-Maqrizi, Khitat, I, 68, recognized the obstacle presented by the Egyptian army, composed of several regiments of white troops amounting to forty thousand horsemen and Sudani foot-soldiers amounting to thirty thousand troops. His source was al-Qadi al-Fadil, then director of the *diwan al-jaysh*. The first figure must evidently include many thousands of Arab auxiliaries. The hostility of the Egyptian troops to the Syrians is vividly portrayed by 'Imad ad-Din, *apud* Abu Shama, I, 162.

already had enough regular troops of his own to decimate them and to drive them out of Cairo into Upper Egypt, where, in the course of the next five years, his brothers gradually crushed their risings.[1]

The white troops made no move and seem to have cooperated with Saladin in repelling Amalric's attacks on Damietta and in the raid on Gaza[2] and the subsequent capture of Aila in December 1170. But Nur ad-Din was pressing him to take the decisive step of proclaiming the 'Abbasid Caliphate in Egypt,[3] and at length in June 1171 sent him a formal order to do so, at the same time notifying the caliph himself of his action.[4] The order was obeyed,

---

1. In 1171 and 1172 Turanshah defeated the Sudanis in Upper Egypt and in 1173 captured the town of Ibrim. They rose again at Aswan 1174, and were put down by his brother al-'Adil, and again defeated at Koptos in 1176. At the same time expeditions were sent out across North Africa as far as Tripoli under Qaraqush.

2. William of Tyre, ed. Salloch, Leipzig, 1934, XX, 21 (trans., II, 376) asserts of the Gaza raid that 'at no time had so great a host of Turks assembled. According to reports, the number of knights alone was about forty thousand.' It is obvious that, allowing for the exaggeration, Saladin must have employed the Egyptian army as well as his own troops on this occasion. On the occasion of a general review held in September 1171, the number of troops in his cavalry regiments (excluding the Arabs) was officially recorded as fourteen thousand (Al-Maqrizi, *Khitat*, I, 86, quoting the diaries of al-Qadi al-Fadil).

3. Shirkuh had already been urged by 'Imad ad-Din to restore the 'Abbasid khutba, in a poetical epistle of congratulation quoted by Abu Shama, I, 160, 7. On Saladin's steps to prepare the ground, see Ibn Abi Tayyi', *apud* Abu Shama, I, 193 and 196, II., 13-21, and 'Imad ad-Din, ibid., 191 (Ibn al-Athir, I, 240). But there is a hint in a later dispatch (Abu Shama, I, 243, 16) of the conflict of conscience that his vizierate involved.

4. 'Imaad ad-Din, who was at that time Nur ad-Din secretary, states positively (Abu Shama, I, 198–9) that Nur ad-Din, having the utmost confidence in Saladin's loyalty and obedience, sent his instructions in Shawwal 566 (June 1171) and at the same time a public announcement of the change and a letter to the caliph. The text of the announcement was drawn up by 'Imad ad-Din himself, and was carried by Shihab ad-Din Ibn Abi 'Asrun, with instructions to read it in every city on his way to Baghdad; it is quoted by Abu Shama, 197–8 (from the chronicle of Ibn Abi Tayyi'), and it confirms =

with no immediate outward disturbances. On al-'Adid's death shortly afterwards the members of the Fatimid ruling house were placed in honourable captivity and the sexes segregated, so that the race should die out in the natural course of time, and the immense treasures of the palaces were shared between Saladin's officers and Nur ad-Din.

The good relations seemed to have been little strained between Nur ad-Din and his faithful 'viceroy' in Egypt, notwithstanding the failure to join forces during the expedition to Shawbak (Mont Real) in October 1171.[1] Ibn al-Athir takes the opportunity to relate a council of war between Saladin and his father to consider the possibility of an invasion by Nur ad-Din, a typical malicious slander of the kind invented by the historian.[2] Nor does the gift to Nur ad-Din seem insufficient from the palaces of the Fatimid caliph.[3] In his dispatch to the caliph (in

---

= his statement that it notified the caliph of Nur ad-Din's orders to Saladin, without waiting for any report of his action. 'Imad ad-Din then goes on to say that later on news was received at Damascus on 10 Shawwal (16 June) that the 'Abbasid khutba had been introduced at Alexandria on 7 Ramadan (14 May) and in Cairo on 28 Ramadan (5 June), i.e., before Nur ad-Din's orders had reached Saladin. The caliph was then at the point of death. The precision and authority of 'Imad ad-Din's statement, confirmed by the terms of his dispatch to the caliph, make it difficult to reject it in favour of the livelier verions of the Aleppo and Mosul chroniclers. Furthermore, Ibn al-Jawzi (*Muntazam*, ed. Krenkow, Hyderabad, 1355–6/1938–40, X, 237, 3) dates the arrival of Ibn Abi 'Asrun in Baghdad on Saturday, 22 Muharram 567 (26 September 1171) with the report that 'the Khalifa had been prayed for in Egypt', which is clearly irreconcilable with the statement that the 'Abbasid khutba was introduced only on the 10th of the same month.

1. The main accusations to the contrary are made by Ibn Abi Tayyi' *apud* Abu Shama, I, 173, and are pointedly rejected by Abu Shama who, rightly, charges Ibn Abi Tayyi' with hostility to Nur ad-Din because of his measures against the Shi'a and the historian's family at Aleppo.

2. Ibn al-Athir does not suggest any breach between them until the first Shawbak expedition of 567/1171, following this up by the recital of Saladin and the amirs (*History of the Atabegs*, R.H.C., Or., II, 68; Kamil, XI, 244–5).

3. Ibn Abi Tyyi' (*apud* Abu Shama, I, 199 inf.) states that Saladin found =

1172 or 1173) Nur ad-Din took the credit for the consequences in Nubia and in North Africa.[1] Ibn al-Athir's subsequent accusation of Saladin's pointed withdrawal from a concerted plan for the siege of Karak on Nur ad-Din's advance is a further example of irresponsible action on his part.[2] On Ibn al-Athir's own dating, Saladin marched into Syria in Shawwal 568 (May–June 1173) and laid siege to Karak; on receiving the news, Nur ad-Din equipped his forces to join Saladin, but the latter slipped away. The date is put a little later by William of Tyre[3] (in July) but he fully confirms 'Imad ad-Din's account and that contained in al-Qadi al-Fadil's dispatch to Nur ad-Din,[4] that it was simply a police operation directed at clearing the bedouin Arabs out of the region and destroying their plantations and to prevent them from assisting the Franks as guides. Furthermore, Ibn al-Athir had himself just related that in June 1173 Nur ad-Din was engaged in a lengthy campaign against the Seljuq Qilij Arslan in the north.[5] It is not surprising that Abu Shama omits his usual citation of Ibn al-Athir's narrative in reference to Saladin's expedition.

At root, any differences between them lay, more probably, in a divergence of political views. Nur ad-Din regarded Syria as the main battlefield against the Crusaders, and looked to Egypt first as a source of revenue to meet the expenses of the *jihad*, and

---

= little money in the Fatimid treasury, 'because Shawar had spent it all in repeated payments to the Franks'.

1. In his dispatch to the caliph, Nur ad-Din took to himself the credit for the conquests in both Nubia and North Africa (Abu Shama, I, 215).

2. *Kamil*, XI, 258–9. It is interesting that this episode is not mentioned in the *Atabegs*, R.H.C., Or., II, 2, 292–3.

3. William of Tyre, XX, 28, trans., II, 389–90.

4. Abu Shama, I, 206.

5. Ibn al-Athir, XI, 257–8; cf. Abu Shama, I, 213 and 'Imad ad-Din *apud* Abu Shama, 215, foot; also *Chronique de Michel le Syrien* (Patriarche d'Antioche 1160–99), ed. J. B. Chabot, Paris, 1899–1910, III, 350.

secondly as a source of additional manpower. Saladin, on the other hand, judging from the former competition for Egypt and the attempt on Damietta in 1169, and probably informed of the tenor of Amalric's negotiations with the Greek emperor in 1171, seems to have been convinced that, for the time being at least, the main point of danger lay in Egypt. Furthermore, he was more conscious than Nur ad-Din could be of the dangers arising from the hostility of the former Fatimid troops and their readiness to make a common cause with the Franks. In his view, therefore, it was his first duty to build up a strong force, to hold Egypt in all contingencies, and to spend what resources he could command on this object. There were also reasons of internal security, illustrated by the fact that he had sent troops to Upper Egypt, and later on to the province of Yemen, which had been a Fatimid stronghold until Turanshah attacked and captured the towns in the early part of 1174.[1] To the end of his life the defence of Egypt against attack remained one of Saladin's constant preoccupations.[2]

That there was, about this time, talk of some kind of action by Nur ad-Din is confirmed by Saladin's explicit denial of the distorted version current in Mosul, in a conversation with Baha' ad-Din: 'Some reports reached us of a possibility that Nur ad-Din might come down to Egypt against us. All our friends were of the opinion that we should oppose him and break off our

---

1. Al-Qadi al-Fadil's dispatch to Nur ad-Din after the attempted Fatimid rising in 1174: Abu Shama, I, 220.

2. The influence of the Fatimid propaganda in Yemen is explicitly offered by Saladin himself as a reason for the expedition to Yemen in his letter of 585/ 1189 to the Almohad Abu Yusuf Ya'qub; see *Mélanges René Basset*, II Paris, 1925, 282. Ibn al-Athir's explanation that Saladin was exploring possible bolt-holes in case of a conflict with Nur ad-Din (an improbable suggestion in any circumstances) displays a typical lack of effort to appreciate the actual situation with which he was confronted in Egypt between 1171 and 1174.

allegiance to him, and I was the only one to hold the opposite view, saying nothing of this kind must ever be said, but the controversy continued until we heard of his death'.[1] Nevertheless, Nur ad-Din's growing exasperation at Saladin's delay in supplying him with funds for *jihad*[2] is explicitly asserted by 'Imad ad-Din[3] and his jealousy might well have been aroused by extravagant panegyrics addressed to 'the kings of the House of Shadhi'. Nur ad-Din, it may be remarked, was not a favourite with the poets, because of his niggardly rewards.[4] However, whatever further plans he may have had in view were cut short by his death on 15 May 1174.

The chief officers of Nur ad-Din's army at once entered into competition for the guardianship of his young son al-Malik as-Salih. Saladin could not remain indifferent to this outbreak of rivalries, but for the time being he took no action beyond acknowledging as-Salih as his suzerain.[5]

In June Amalric laid siege to Banyas, but Saladin, having received warning from Constantinople to expect an attack by the Sicilian fleet, was unable to move.[6] It was not until the end of July that the naval assault on Alexandria was made and beaten off, and in the meantime the situation in Syria had taken a grave turn. The amirs of Damascus had made a separate peace

---

1. Baha', Schultens, 50 = Cairo, 37.
2. 'Imad ad-Din's report of his statement to Nur ad-Din's commissioner (Abu Shama, I, 219, 22–5): 'A province of this size cannot be adequately guarded without heavy expenditure.'
3. 'Imad ad-Din (in Abu Shama, 206) conveys Nur ad-Din's growing exasperation at Saladin's delay in supplying him with funds for the *jihad*.
4. Abu Shama, I, 200 foot; Nur ad-Din's parsimony with the poets, ibid., 229.
5. Dispatch, cited by Abu Shama, I, 230.
6. He was encamped at the time at the frontier station of Faqus, to which he had advanced his troops on learning of the Crusaders' attack on Banyas: 'Imad, *apud* Abu Shama, I, 231 (cf. Ibn Abi Tayyi', ibid., 222, 14) and 235, 7.

with Jerusalem on payment of tribute;[1] Nur ad-Din's cousin at Mosul had invaded and annexed all his provinces beyond the Euphrates; and in August the eunuch Gumushtagin, having secured the person of as-Salih, established himself at Aleppo and threw Nur ad-Din's lieutenants into his dungeons. The unity of Islam in the face of the Crusaders was disrupted. In reply to Saladin's remonstrances and hints of intervention, the amirs appealed to him to be loyal to the house that had raised him up. His answer was categorical: 'In the interests of Islam and its people we put first and foremost whatever will combine their forces and unite them in one purpose; in the interests of the House of Atabeg we put first and foremost whatever will safeguard its root and its branch. Loyalty can only be the consequence of loyalty. We are in one valley and those who think ill of us are in another.'[2] It was therefore with full consciousness of his mission as the true heir of Nur ad-Din that he set himself to rebuild the shattered edifice of his empire and, on an urgent appeal from the commandant at Damascus, occupied it, almost without opposition, on 28 October 1174.[3]

Fully justified as Saladin's action was both to himself and in

---

1. In a letter to the Qadi of Aleppo, the famous Ibn Abi 'Asrun, cited by Ibn Abi Tayyi' (Abu Shama, I, 233), Saladin makes it plain that his chief grievance against the amirs of Damascus was that this armistice freed the Crusaders to attack the Muslims on other fronts.

2. 'Imad, *apud* Abu Shama, I, 234.

3. Ibn al-Athir, XI, 275, stresses the smallness of the forces that accompanied Saladin on this occasion: seven hundred horsemen only. No figure is quoted in Abu Shama's abridgment of 'Imad (I, 236); but the succeeding events make Ibn al-Athir's statement more deserving of credence than Baha's description of his assembling of 'a great force of troops' (Schultens, 42 = Cairo, 38–9). Ibn Abi Tayyi' (*apud* Abu Shama, I, 237 foot) describes the general attitude of the people of Damascus towards Saladin as one of strong support, and although his evidence on such a point is suspect (see above) it agrees with all the indications contained in the sources.

the light of history, his contemporaries and rivals could not be expected to see it in the same light. In their eyes, naturally enough, he was only one of themselves, and presumably inspired by the same motives of self-interest and lust for power, cloak them as he might by high-sounding appeal to the principles and interests of Islam.[1] His occupation of Damascus seemed only a clever move to forestall them. When he appointed his brother Tughtagin as its governor, and himself pressed northwards in December with a small force to occupy Hims and Hamah and to demand that Aleppo should open its gates to him as the rightful guardian of as-Salih, they concluded that he was bent upon nothing but the aggrandizement of his own house at the expense of the house of Zangi.

This is the view of Saladin which is presented by the Mosul chronicler, and it was the view of as-Salih himself, who appealed to the population of Aleppo to protect him from his self-appointed deliverer.[2] The amirs had recourse to the familiar expedients: the hiring of *fida'is* from Sinan, the 'Old Man of the Mountains', to assassinate Saladin, an agreement with Raymond of Tripoli that in return for favours past and to come he should create a diversion by attacking Hims, and an appeal to Mosul in the name of family solidarity.[3] The attempted assassination

---

1. See Ibn Abi Tayyi''s account of his interview with the envoy of the Nuriya of Aleppo, Qutb ad-Din Yanal, *apud* Abu Shama, I, 237–8, and the concordant narrative (in this case at second-hand) of 'Imad, ibid., 240 sup.

2. Ibn al-Athir (XI, 276–7) naturally omits from his narrative the details of the concessions made to the Shi'ites of Aleppo in return for their support: see Ibn Abi Tayyi', *apud* Abu Shama, I, 238 foot.

3. Ibn Abi Tayyi' (*apud* Abu Shama, I, 249) states that during his first investment of Aleppo Saladin had sent a detachment of his army to support the Zangid 'Imad ad-Din, who was being besieged by his brother Saif ad-Din of Mosul in Sinjar, and had adhered to Saladin. The relations between 'Imad ad-Din and Saladin are mentioned also by Baha' (Schultens, 44 = Cairo, 40 and Ibn al-Athir (XI, 278) but neither refers to military assistance =

failed, but Saladin withdrew to defend Hims.[1] Two months later, in face of the combined forces of Mosul and Aleppo, he consented to withdraw from northern Syria and content himself with holding Damascus as the lieutenant of as-Salih. The allies then tried to press their advantage, and on his refusal to yield further, they attacked, only to be routed at the Horns of Hamah, thanks to the timely arrival of the Egyptian regiments.[2] When Saladin posted his forces around Aleppo for the second time, Gumushtagin had no alternative but to accept his terms, which left Aleppo in the hands of as-Salih on the condition that the two armies should combine in operations against the Franks.[3]

=   from Saladin to 'Imad ad-Din. On his relations with the Assassins, see B. Lewis, 'Saladin and the Assassins' in *B. S. O. A. S.*, XV, 1953, 239–45.

1.   According to William of Tyre (XXI, 8; trans., II, 410), Saladin, after his capture of the citadel of Hims (which he had merely masked on his rapid advance), released the hostages held there as guarantee for the execution of the terms on which Raymond had been released by Nur ad-Din, and did so in return for an undertaking by Raymond not to intervene in this conflict with Aleppo. But as William of Tyre places the capture of the citadel after the battle of the Horns of Hamah, whereas 'Imad (on this occasion an eyewitness) dates it exactly on 17 March (*apud* Abu Shama, I, 245), and the battle took place on 13 April, it seems probable that his statement is to be connected with the armistice that Saladin concluded with Raymond in the course of the summer ('Imad, *apud* Abu Shama, I, 252). The intermediary was Humphrey of Toron (William of Tyre, loc. cit.) whom Syrian tradition credited with having knighted Saladin at some earlier time (see Lane-Poole, 91).

2.   Ibn Abi Tayyi' (*apud* Abu Shama, I, 250) attributes the victory of Saladin partly to a previous understanding between him and certain elements in the '*askar* of Aleppo; so also William of Tyre (XXI, 8; trans., II, 410). *Michel le syrien*, III, 366, makes a similar statement concerning the engagement in the following year, but of the generals in the '*askar* of Mosul.

3.   Ibn Abi Tayyi' (*apud* Abu Shama, I, 250) states as the terms of the agreement that when as-Salih should go out against any enemy Saladin and his armies would join him, that the *khutba* should remain unchanged, and the coinage be struck in the name of as-Salih. But al-Fadil's dispatch to Baghdad in the following year gives as the substance of the agreement that the army of Aleppo should be employed in operations (*bikarat*) against the infidels (Abu Shama, 254). Ibn al-Athir (XI, 279) states that as-Salih's name was dropped from the *khutba* and coinage during this investment of Aleppo.

This was at the end of April 1175. A few days later, at Hamah, the envoys from the caliph brought his formal investiture with the government of Egypt and Syria.[1] For most princes of his time this investiture was a mere formality but for Saladin it was much more. If the war to which he had vowed himself against the Crusaders was to be a real *jihad*, a true 'Holy War', it was imperative to conduct it with scrupulous observance of the revealed Law of Islam. A government that sought to serve the cause of God in battle must be not only a lawful government, duly authorized by the supreme representative of the Divine Law, but must serve God with equal zeal in its administration and in its treatment of its subjects. In brief, Saladin's object was to restore to Islamic politics the reign of law, a concept that had become for the contemporary princes not only an empty phrase but an absurdity. Already, during his first years in Egypt and following the example set by Nur ad-Din, he had abolished all forms of taxation that were contrary to Islamic Law, and his first action in Damascus was to abolish them there. This became his invariable practice on each addition to his territories, and was stipulated formally in the diplomas issued to his vassals.[2] It is

---

1. The text of the diploma investing him with the whole of Syria (in addition to Egypt and Yemen) 'except what is in the hand of Nur ad-Din Isma'il son of Nur ad-Din Mahmud, namely Aleppo and its dependencies', quoted in Qalqashandi, *Subh al-A'sha*, ed. Cairo 1913–19, X, 135–44. This was composed by Diya'ad-Din Ibn al-Athir and betrays the family's nervous fear and suspicion of Saladin.

2. The preamble to the decree abolishing illegal dues in Egypt published on 3 Safar 567 (8 October 1171), quoted by Abu Shama (I, 205), shows this idea already present: 'We praise God for that He has established us firmly in the land, and has made agreeable to us the performance of every duty, whether supererogatory or obligatory, and has raised us up to remove from amongst His creatures whatsoever intrudes upon the worship of Him, and has chosen us to engage in the Holy War on behalf of God in the true sense of the term *al-jihad fi'llahi haqqa jihadihi* and has made us to esteem little the paltry goods of this world ...' The list of *Mukus* affected by the decree is given =

true that they did not always observe the condition but an offender was liable to find himself summarily dispossessed of his government in consequence.[1] The duty of the ruler, he asserted over and over again, was to be 'the protector of the Faith and the guardian of the property of the Muslims' and he rebuked his brother al-'Adil for thinking that 'countries are to be bought and sold.'[2]

The sources vividly portray the repeated amazement of his officers and subjects that the personal acquisitions and exercise of power which were the first objects of most princes and governors - including those of his own house - were of no interest to him, and that wealth was a thing to be used in prosecution of the Holy War or to be given to others.[3] The fact was patent even to the Crusaders. As early as 1175, when

---

= by al-Maqrizi, *Khitat*, I, 104–5 (ed. Wiet, II, 1, 81–6, where the editor points out that about the same time Nur ad-Din abolished the *Mukus* at Damascus - actually some years earlier, see Abu Shama, I, 15, where Saladin supports Nur ad-Din against the strong criticism and opposition to this measure of Shirkuh at Hamah). Other instances of Saladin's abolition of *Mukus*: at Damascus, on his occupation, Abu Shama, I, 235, 237; at Aleppo, ibid., II, 47 ('Imad, *Barq*, V, f. 87, contains the text of a dispatch on this subject by 'Imad); at Mecca, ibid., I, 270; at Rahba, ibid., II, 69, with an important quotation from the rescript representing this as his general policy. Cf. also the conditions of which Nur ad-Din Qara-Asrlan was invested with Amid: 'Imad *apud* Abu Shama, II, 44 ('Imad, *Barq*, V, f. 37a), and generally in all other investitures. The same theme appears over and over again in his correspondence with the caliph's *diwan* at Baghdad, and in passages relating to the government of his deputies, e. go, 'Imad, *fath*, 125. On the parallel development of the idea of *jihad* and orthodoxy and good government under Nur ad-Din and Saladin, see E. Sivan, *L'Islam et la croisade*, Paris, 1968, 59–130.

1. Removel of Abu'l-Haija' from Nasibin, Abu Shama, II, 3 (Ibn al-Athir, XI, 322, expands this notice with a characteristic twist).
2. Ibn Abi Tayyi', *apud* Abu Shama, II, 52.
3. Cf 'Imad's conclusion of his narrative of the capture of Amid: 'I have set out this story in detail in order that you may know that the world held no place in the sultan's scale of values' ('Imad, *Barq*, V, f. 65a: and Baha', Schultens, 12–13 = Cairo, 10–13).

Raymond agreed to terms with Aleppo in order to draw off Saladin, William of Tyre observed that 'any increase of Saladin's power was cause for suspicion in our eyes ... For he was a man wise in counsel, valiant in war, and generous beyond measure. It seemed wiser to us to lend aid to the boy king ... not for his own sake, but to encourage him as an adversary against Saladin.'[1]

No greater justification than this could well be found for the policy that Saladin had adopted. Eight years later he used the same argument in an outspoken dispatch to the Caliphate:

> Your servant believes that there is no stratagem more fraught with mischief for the enemy and the infidel, no effort more effective against the misguided, no favour more profitable in stirring up the anger of the leaders of heresy, than to enlarge your servant's power to increase his opportunity of service. For let it be considered, is there amongst all the rulers of Islam another one whose extension of power is a source of grief and affliction to the infidels?[2]

But the facts were not so patent at Mosul, where the terms of the agreement with Aleppo, and probably also the diploma from the caliph, were received with incredulous anger. It was not only that a prince of the Zangid house was reduced virtually to a vassal of one of his father's creatures. What was still more disagreeable was that the creature was a Kurd, who challenged the Turkish monopoly of sovereignty, now established for a century and a half, and bestowed his conquests upon his own kinsmen. It was indeed the hardest task with which Saladin was

---

1. William of Tyre, XXI, c. 6 (trans., II, 405–6), cf. *Michel le syrien*, III, 365, where the Jacobite patriarch records his chivalrous conduct towards defeated troops of Mosul, and his lavish gifts of money to the troops in Syria.
2. Dispatch of al-Qadi al-Fadil after the capture of Amid in 579/1183, *apud* Abu Shama, II, 40.

faced to overcome the professional jealousy of the Turkish officers. It delayed his occupation of Aleppo for six years, and made its embarrassing influence felt throughout the Third Crusade. Ibn al-Athir vividly represents it in repeating the indignant words of one of his Mosul compatriots, as he watched Saladin being assisted onto his horse during the defence of Jerusalem: 'Have a care son of Ayyub, what sort of death you will come to – you who are helped to mount by a Seljuq prince and a descendant of the atabeg Zangi!'[1]

To what extent, indeed, personal motives were mingled with Saladin's genuine devotion to the cause and ideals of Islam is a question that it may never be possible to resolve. But in the circumstances of the time, however un-self-regarding his motives were, the only way in which his objectives could be realized was by concentrating power in his own hands, and establishing in all key positions persons on whose loyalty he could count with absolute assurance. This meant first and foremost the members of his own family, and after them such of his Mamluk or Kurdish generals and of the vassal princes who had proved themselves trustworthy. The attitude of the Zangids themselves drove him in the same direction, when he had learned the futility of relying upon alliances and confederations.

Before leaving northern Syria, Saladin sent his troops to raid the Isma'ili territories in Jabal as-Summaq[2] then withdrew to Damascus, where he made a truce with Jerusalem. An envoy had been sent to Mosul to ensure Saif ad-Din's acceptance of the agreement, and had obtained satisfactory assurances. When,

---

1. Ibn al-Athir, XII, 50. Cf. the remarks attributed to the troops of Mosul by Michael, *Michel le syrien*, III, 365.
2. Sibt b. al-Jawzi, *Mir'at az-Zaman*, ed. Jewett, New York, 1907. See Lewis, 'Saladin and the Assassins', 240–1.

however, the envoy of Mosul in turn came to Damascus to swear Saladin to its terms, he presented in error a document that provided for an offensive alliance between Mosul and Aleppo.[1] Saladin was prepared, therefore, when, in April 1176 the allies mustered their forces again. Marching northwards, he met them on the 22nd at Tall as-Sultan, fifteen miles from Aleppo, and drove them in headlong flight from the field.[2] Restraining his army from pursuit, he distributed amongst them the immense booty, released the captives, and sent back to Saif ad-Din the cages of doves, nightingales, and parrots found in his canteen with an ironic message to amuse himself with them and keep out of military adventures in future. The disgusted Sultan, says the contemporary Aleppo chronicler, 'found the Mosul camp more like a tavern, with all its wines, guitars, lutes, bands, singers, and singing girls, and showing it to his troops prayed that they might be preserved from such an affliction.'[3]

---

1. Abu Shama, I, 253 and dispatch of al-Qadi al-Fadil (ibid., 254).
2. Ibn Abi Tayyi' (*apud* Abu Shama, I, 260–7) gives the chief credit for the victory to Saladin's brother Shams al-Dawla Turanshah, who had returned from Yemen to Damascus only three days before (7 Shawwal = 19 April: 'Imad *apud* Abu Shama, 259, 26), apparently by a confusion of Turanshah with Farrukhshah (cf 'Imad *apud* Abu Shama, 254 foot and 256, 5). Tuanshah had in fact remained in Damascus as its governor, with instructions to prevent Frankish incursions during the campaign in the north (Ibn Abi Tayyi', *apud* Abu Shama, I, 260, 8), and 'Imad asserts positively that Saladin and Turanshah met, for the first time since the latter's expedition to Yemen, at Hamah on 2 Safar (10 August): Abu Shama, 261 foot. Ibn al-Athir's account of the battle (XI, 283) is highly artificial, to the point of asserting that only one man was killed, and he finds a scapegoat in Saif ad-Din's favourite Zulfandar.
3. Ibn Abi Tayyi', *apud* Abu Shama, I, 255. Although such anecdotal embellishments are suspect on principle, the last part is clearly not an invention. In the same spirit 'Imad, as an eyewitness, contrasts the sobriety and discipline of Saladin's troops at the siege of Sinjar in 578/1182 with the laxity and disorder of the troops of Diyar Bakr: 'Imad, *Barq*, V, f. 17b.

In spite of Saladin's magnanimity Aleppo still held out,[1] but when, after storming its protecting fortresses to the east and north, Buza'a, Manbij and 'Azaz, he again invested it on 26 June, its defenders consented to a renewal of the arrangement made the year before, and a general peace was signed a month later between Saladin, his brother Turanshah at Damascus, the princes of Aleppo and Mosul, and the Artuqid vassals of Mosul (the princes of Hiss Kaifa and Mardin), all parties swearing to join together against any one of them who should break the agreement.[2] The alliance was formally ratified by an exchange of envoys in the course of the year. As-Salih regained 'Azaz on the intercession of his little sister, and undertook to give Saladin the assistance of the army of Aleppo should he require it.[3]

---

1. The resistance of the Nuriya at Aleppo was presumably stiffened by expectation of the assistance on 'guarantee' of which Reynald and Joscelin had been released on the arrival of the Mosul forces at Aleppo ('Imad *apud* Abu Shama, I, 255 top; cf. William of Tyre, XXI, 11 (trans. II, 414)). It is possible also that they had information of the impending raid by Baldwin IV on the Biqa' at the beginning of August, of which Saladin had warned his brother Turanshah (see n. 2 above). Cf 'Imad's account of the raid, the riposte of Ibn al-Muqaddam from Ba'albak, and the reverse suffered by Turanshah at 'Ain al-Jarr (*apud* Abu Shama, 261 inf.) with William of Tyre, loc. cit. (trans., II, 412–13), where the mention of Shams ad-Dawla proves that the correct date is 1176, not 1175 as stated in the note on p. 412.

2. The date of the agreement is given only by Kamal ad-Din (*Zubdat al-halab*, ed. S. Dahhan, Damascus, 1954–67, III, 29–30; tr. Blocher, *Revue de l'orient latin*, III, Paris, 1895, 58): 16 Muharram = 25/6 July. Ibn al-A'thir's date, 20 Muharram (XI, 285–6), is apparently due to a misreading of the date given by 'Imad (*apud* Abu Shama, I, 261, 27) for Saladin's departure from Aleppo.

3. The terms of the treaty are given by 'Imad (*apud* Abu Shama, I, 261) but without mention of the condition requiring the services of the army at Aleppo. This is expressly stated by Baha' (Schultens, 47 = Cairo, 13) in reference to the presence of the troops of Aleppo under his command on the expedition into Cilicia in 1180. The exchanges of embassies in 572/1176–7 are mentioned by 'Imad in Ibn Abi Tayyi', *apud* Abu Shama, 269. It is to be noted that Saladin's brother Turanshah, the governor of Damascus, was a separate party to the treaty, since Saladin had apparently given him a free hand at Damascus (see n. 3, below), as were also the Artuqid vassals of Mosul.

During the siege of 'Azaz, a second and still more determined attempt had been made on Saladin's life by emissaries of the Assassins. On his return from Aleppo, therefore, he marched on Misyaf, the Syrian headquarters of the sect, and laid siege to it, while his troops ravaged the neighbourhood. What followed is largely enveloped in legend; but Saladin withdrew to Damascus and dismissed his Egyptian forces to their homes. The only certain thing is that for the rest of his life he had nothing to fear from the Assassins.

After marrying at Damascus the widow of Nur ad-Din[1] Saladin returned to Egypt, which had been governed in his absence by his brother al-'Adil, and occupied himself for a year in internal affairs. His restless brother Turanshah, who had returned from the Yemen on learning of the Syrian conquests, had been left at Damascus as governor with full powers,[2] and its former governor Ibn al-Muqaddam was recompensed with Ba'albak. Hims was governed by his maternal uncle Mahmud ibn Takush, and Hamah by Shirkuh's son Nasir ad-Din. His nephew Tapi ad-Din 'Umar, the most warlike and impetuous member of the family, who had watched with a jealous eye the distribution of kingdoms and governments to his relatives, was still engaged in attempting to carve out a kingdom for himself in the west. In 1175 his Armenian mamluk Sharaf ad-Din Qaraqush captured Augila, and a second expedition sent out in 1176, in spite of al-'Adil's protests, occupied Fezzan.[3] It was one of the weaknesses

---

1. Before leaving Damascus Saladin 'legitimated' his succession by marrying 'Ismat ad-Din, the daughter of its last independent prince Mu'in ad-Din Unar (the pronouncement is given by 'Imad) and widow of his successor Nur ad-Din: 'Imad *apud* Abu Shama, I, 263 foot.

2. See 'Imad, *Barq*, III, 25a: وهو متصرّف فيها تصرّف المالك ; also 'Imad, *Barq*, III, 120a: عوّل على هذا أخيه . . . بالشام في السلطنة . . . وفوّض إليه الأمر وولاّه تولية مطلقة.

3. Ibn Abi Tayyi' *apud* Abu Shama, I, 260, 269–70. For the raids of 575/1179, ibid. II, 16; of 577/1181, ibid., II, 27; and the capitulation of Tripoli =

of Saladin, which was to lead him into many embarrassments, that he found it difficult to restrain the appetites of his kinsmen. Taqi ad-Din's raids into the west continued for some years and led eventually to a clash with the forces of the Almohad sultan of Morocco. Saladin, so far as the evidence goes, took no hand in organizing them, but he certainly connived at them and even took credit for them in his dispatches to Baghdad.[1] The time was to come, at a critical juncture in the Third Crusade, when in his urgent need of the help of the Almohads, he would do his best to repudiate responsibility for them.[2] His chief attention was directed to the construction of the citadel and the great walls of Cairo, which he had begun in 1171 as a precaution against future Frankish invasions, together with the reorganization of the fleet.[3] At the same time he was earnestly concerned to foster in Egypt the orthodox reform movement which had grown up in Syria under Nur ad-Din's government, and both he and al-'Adil set the example of founding the new colleges from which it was diffused.

In August 1177, the news of the arrival in Palestine of Philip of Flanders gave the signal for fresh preparations for war. Whether

---

= and invasion of Ifriqiya in 578/1182, ibid., II, 38. It is noteworthy that Ibn Abi Tayyi' is the source of all these notices, and that he confuses Taqi ad-Din's Armenian general Sharaf ad-Din Qaraqush with Saladin's intendant Baha' ad-Din Qaraqush.

1. See, for example, 'Imad, *apud* Abu Shama, II, 17.

2. See Gaudefroy-Demombynes, 'Une Lettre de Saladin au calife Almohade' in *Mélanges René Basset*, II, Paris, 1925, pp. 289–305.

3. Details of measures for expansion of the fleet are given from Ibn Abi Tayyi', *apud* Abu Shama, I, 269 sup. al-Muqrizi (*Suluk*, I, 73) states under date 577/1181–2 that Saladin 'fixed the appointments [*qarrara*] of the *diwan* of the Fleet, to include the Fayyum, the Juyushi *waqf* [336–0], *al-kharaji* [?], and the *natrun* [Ibn Mammati, 334–6] and the *kharaj* was leased [*dumina*] for 8,000 dinars'. Ibn Mammati, p. 341, states that certain estates were assigned for the expenses of the wall and citadel, and the officials were authorized to demand the materials required for their construction.

or not he was informed of the proposals made to Philip to invade Egypt, it was a condition of the truce with the Franks that 'if any king or great noble arrived they were free to give him assistance, and the armistice should be renewed on his withdrawal.'[1] The first attack in the new campaign, that made on Hamah in October, was repulsed by local troops and volunteers under the command of Saif ad-Din al-Mashtub.[2] As the Crusaders moved up to besiege Harim, Saladin planned a large-scale raid on Ascalon and Gaza. On this occasion he seems to have thought it safe to engage a larger proportion than hitherto of the Egyptian forces on the raid.[3] 'Imad ad-Din gives a vivid picture of the light-hearted confidence of the Egyptian troops as they assembled at the advanced base and as they dispersed on plundering raids over the countryside. Baldwin IV's vigorous counteraction, and well-timed surprise attack on the regiment of guards at Mont Gisard near Ramla on 25 November, threw the whole force into confusion, and the remnants struggled back to

---

1. 'Imad, *Barq*, III, f. 25b, quoted Abu Shama, I, 275. He adds that the attack on Hamah was not, therefore, a breach of the truce.

2. 'Imad, loc. cit.: *ijtama'a ilaiha rijal ut-ta'ni wad-darb*. Ibn al-Athir (XI, 294) mistakenly places this event after the disaster at Ramla, and represents it as the consequence of the temporary disablement of Saladin.

3. William of Tyre, XXI, c. 23 (trans, II, 430–1), estimates Saladin's forces at eight thousand toassin (*tawashis*), including Saladin's private guard of one thousand mamluks, and eighteen thousand *qaraghulams*. From the exact figures of the Egyptian forces quoted by Al-Maqrizi (*Khitat*, I, 86, 87) from the diaries of al-Qadi al-Fadil for the years 567/1171 and 577/1181, it is clear that the total number or *tawashis* of regular mamluks in the Egyptian army did not at any time exceed eight thousand and the *qaraghulams* (probably non-Mamluk horsemen) numbered seven thousand at the most, though there may have been some squadrons of Arab cavalry in addition. Since Saladin was able to set out only four months after the disaster with a considerable force, it is evident that by no means the whole of the Egyptian *'askar* was involved at Ramla, nor even (as Ibn al-Athir asserts, XI, 293) the greater part of it. 'Imad's account is given in *Barq*, III, ff. 5 sqq., and summarized by Abu Shama, I, 271–3.

Egypt as best they could, harassed by the Franks and the bedouins and by lack of both food and water. To Saladin himself, who owed his escape to the foresight and loyalty of al-Qadi al-Fadil, it was a lesson that he never forgot.

Nevertheless, so far from decisive was the defeat that only four months later he was able to set out again with a refitted army, and yet leave sufficient forces behind to guard the security of Egypt.[1] The expedition this time was to be no mere raid, but had the definite object of attacking the Frankish forces besieging Harim, and although Saladin was forestalled in this by the raising of the siege on payment of an indemnity by the government of Aleppo,[2] he pushed on to Hims and encamped there in readiness to take the field at the first opportunity. The withdrawal of the count of Flanders automatically brought the armistice into effect again; in addition, a bad year had brought severe scarcity in Syria. Yet Saladin was eager to resume the *jihad*, and although all the eloquence of al-Fadil was exerted to persuade him to hold his hand until conditions were more favourable, he was already assuring the caliph's ministers that, if all went well and if the troops duly mustered, he would attack Jerusalem in the following year.[3]

---

1. Saladin's military and naval measures for the defence of Egypt before setting out in March 1178 are detailed in a dispatch written by 'Imad to Baghdad, quoted in *Barq*, III, f. 45b. That the object of the expedition was to attack the Crusaders who were besieging Harim is definitely asserted by him, f. 28b, and in the same and other dispatches, ff. 42a and 42b. Kamal ad-Din (III, 32; Blochet, 64) says that the hard-pressed garrison of Harim had called on Saladin to defend them.

2. Cf. William of Tyre, XXI, 25 (trans., II, 435). 'Imad in a dispatch to Baghdad (*Barq*, III, f. 42b), points to the truce arranged between Aleppo and the Crusaders on learning of Saladin's arrival in Syria as resulting from a common interest. *Michel le syrien*, III, 376, states the amount paid by al-Malik as-Salih to 'the prince' as 20,000 dinars.

3. 'Imad, *Barq*, III, ff. 37–40, 46, 63 sqq., contains extracts from the correspondence between Saladin and al-Qadi al-Fadil during this period; =

In August, the Franks broke the armistice by an attack on Hamah. It was driven off without much difficulty, and the prisoners were brought to Saladin, who ordered their execution for breach of faith. A more serious breach occured when Baldwin began the construction of a fortress at Jacob's Ford, at the instance of the Templars, in October.[1] But Saladin was unable to intervene at the moment owing to a delicate situation that had arisen at Damascus. His brother Turanshah had completely neglected his duties as governor,[2] besides being on suspiciously good terms with as-Salih at Aleppo.[3] The sultan had accordingly appointed his nephew Farrukhshah as military commandant at Damascus. Turanshah now demanded that he should be given the fief of Ba'albak, which was held by the former governor of Damascus, Ibn al-Muqaddam. Very unwillingly, and only after vain efforts to prevent a clash by dissuading his brother or persuading Ibn al-Muqaddam to accept another fief, Saladin consented to the investment of Ba'albak during his absence in the north, but endeavoured to limit military action against Ibn al-Muqaddam to a minimum. On his return from Hims his full forces encamped round Ba'albak for some weeks, but when winter set in they were disbanded

---

= cf. Abu Shama, I, 276; II, 2–3. In the first letter the Qadi refers to a Frankish attack on Sadr, on the Egyptian border. The dispatch to the caliph's *diwan* was written by 'Imad, *Barq*, III, 43 ab.

1. Ernoul, 52, asserts definitely Baldwin's reluctance to undertake this construction in time of truce, and that Saladin tried to dissuade him from it. Saladin's offer of 60,000 and finally of 100,000 gold pieces to him if he would abandon the plan is related by both Ibn Abi Tayyi' (*apud* Abu Shama, II, 8) and 'Imad, *Barq*, III (Abu Shama, II, 11).

2. 'Imad, *Barq*, III, f. 25a (briefly summarized *apud* Abu Shama, I, 275, where in l. 19 *bi-dhatihim* should be corrected to *bi-ladhdhatihim*): ما قد بذل للفرنج [أمنت [أذنت غائص.MS به البلاد من مضراتهم وسلمت به الغلات من غاراتهم وهو خائض في أمره وإنفاذه في بحر ملاذه . . . واشتغل كل من الأمراء . . . بهزله وجدّه.

3. 'Imad, *Barq*, III, f. 120a. جرى شمس الدولة معه [الملك الصالح] على الوفاء والوفاق ونهج سبيل الاشفاق.

except for a small masking force. Eventually Ibn al-Muqaddam yielded and Saladin consented to Turanshah's investment with Ba'albak and when Ibn al-Muqaddam eventually yielded he was given extensive fiefs in the north; the loyal relationship between him and Saladin remained unbroken, and on the death of Farrukhshah in 1183 he was reappointed to the governorship of Damascus. The episode temporarily weakened Saladin's diplomatic position as against his rivals; but in the long run it was largely due to his firm, yet conciliatory, attitude towards Ibn al-Muqaddam in this conflict that he never again had to take military measures against an insubordinate officer.[1]

With this problem out of his way, Saladin was free to resume the offensive in the spring of 1179. He began by reorganizing the commands in the north, appointing Taqi ad-Din to Hamah and Nasir ad-Din ibn Shirkuh to Hims, to hold Raymond of Tripoli in check.[2] A second winter without rains had created famine conditions in Syria, his troops were suffering severely and remonstrated with him, but he answered only 'God will provide' and sent the most incapacitated back to Egypt with Turanshah, asking al-'Adil to send him fifteen hundred picked

---

1. The episode is related in detail by 'Imad in *Barq*, III, 62, 102 sqq., Abu Shama, II, 2, 5, and Ibn al-Athir, XI, 298, and briefly in *Michel le syrien*, III, 379, who asserts that Ibn al-Muqaddam sent gifts to the Franks and promised his allegiance to them. But his narrative of events in general is not reliable except in relation to Northern Syria. The acute discomfort that it caused Saladin is reflected in the embarrassment with which he tries to explain his action against Ibn- al-Muqaddam and excuse his failure to resume the *jihad* in his dispatches to the caliph's *diwan*, covering it up by complaints of the obstacles placed in his way by 'kings and sultans' and their failure to support him in his struggles with the Franks ('Imad, *Barq*, 103 b, ff.). Turanshah held Ba'albak only for a year; in 1180 he asked, or was persuaded, to take Alexandria in exchange for it and died there soon afterwards.

2. 'Imad, *apud* Abu Shama, II, 8. With Taqi ad-Din were Ibn al-Muqaddam and Saif ad-Din al-Mashtub, and his second-in-command was Nasir ad-Din Mankurus (*sic*) b. Khumartagin, who held the fief of Abu Qubais.

men in return, along with supplies.[1] Early in April, on receiving reports of a projected raid by Baldwin, he sent out Farrukhshah with the Damascus regiment, numbering about one thousand mamluks, with orders to shadow the Franks, and send back information of their movements. Farrukhshah, however, found himself engaged almost by accident near Belfort, and gained a brilliant success, the more welcome to the Muslims in that the constable Humphrey of Toron was amongst the killed.[2]

Shortly afterwards Saladin moved out to Banyas and, trusting to receive warning from his spies of any concentration of Frankish troops, posted a guard at Tall al-Qadi and dispersed his forces to loot for forage and supplies. Bands of starving Arab tribesmen, who had followed him up, were dispatched into the districts of Sidon and Beirut to reap all the grain that they could find. In the plain of Marj 'Uyun, he was surprised by the appearance of a large force under Baldwin, but hastily mounting all the available troops he turned an initial reverse into a notable victory.[3] The date was the second day of the year 575, 10 June 1179, and 'Imad ad-Din, who drew up the register of the prisoners, relates that over 270 knights were among them, exclusive of lower ranks.

Adequately supplied now for a major operation, Saladin enlisted large auxiliary forces of Turkmen and siege troops to supplement the regiments from the Syrian cities and the fresh

---

1. 'Imad, *apud* Abu Shama, II, 6, from *Barq*, III, 114. In his letter to al-'Adil (ibid., f. 121) Saladin refers to rumours of another project of invasion by the Sicilian fleet, but this may have been only a cover for the return of Turanshah.

2. 'Imad, *Barq*, 116–19 (Abu Shama, II, 6); William of Tyre, XXI, 27 (trans., II, 439). On Humphrey 'Imad says (119a): لقد كان حتف ذلك العظيم فتحاً عظيماً.

3. Full accounts by William of Tyre, XXI, cc. 28–9 (II, 440–43), and 'Imad, *Barq*, III, 124–30 (Abu Shama, II, 8, but briefly) who agree on the general outlines of the events.

Egyptian contingent, and on 25 August invested Jacob's Castle. In order to forestall intervention, the siege was prosecuted with the utmost vigour and resolution. On the sixth day the castle was stormed, the seven hundred defenders taken prisoner, and the Muslim captives released. In spite of the heat and stench of dead bodies, Saladin would not leave until the last stone had been razed, and carried out a series of forays into the territories of Jerusalem before returning to Damascus.[1]

If this succession of Muslim victories left the Franks 'clothed with great fear and confusion', it definitely established Saladin's claim to leadership in the Holy War, not only amongst his own subjects but also at Baghdad, where he had found a firm supporter in the powerful treasurer Zahir ad-Din Ibn al-'Attar.[2] In view not only of the still unresolved conflict with the Zangids, but also of his own principles, the benevolence of the Caliphate was a matter of the first importance to him. From the casual glimpses supplied by the sources, it is evident that a bitter struggle was going on at the caliph's court between the partisans of the Zangids and those of Saladin.[3] At every stage of his career, he felt himself under the necessity of dispatching pleading and argumentative letters to Baghdad, justifying his

---

1. 'Imad, *Barq*, III, ff. 139–43; the summary in Abu Shama, II, 9, is fairly full but omits the reference to the enlistment of the Turkmen; William of Tyre, XXI, 30 (trans., II, 443–4). Apart from al-Fadil's dispatches (Abu Shama, II, 13–14) the other sources contain no material additions; it is from them (p. 13, l. 29) that Abu Shama took the statement about the raids that followed the capture of the castle (p. 11, l. 26) which is not in the extant portion of *al-Barq al-Shami*.

2. 'Imad, *Barq*, III, ff. 40b and 58; Abu Shama, I, 276, 278. It was Zahir ad-Din who established an-Nasir as caliph in succession to al-Mustadi' at the end of March 1180, only to be arrested five days later and put to death: Ibn al-Athir, XI, 304.

3. 'Imad, III, f. 58a, shows also that the time-honoured practice of making lavish gifts to the 'notables, nobles, dignitaries, religious leaders, poets, sufis, etc.' at Baghdad was not neglected.

actions, protesting his loyalty to the Caliphate and the Sacred Law Shari'a, and claiming the caliph's support against his adversaries. From this time, it would seem, and perhaps still more after the accession of an-Nasir as caliph in March 1180, his cause was definitely in the ascendant, although the opposing party fought a long rearguard action, which did not cease even with the victory of Hattin.[1]

Although Saladin was still in treaty relations with Aleppo and Mosul,[2] the Zangids and their vassals had shown no readiness to assist him in the reconquest of Palestine. The modest successes that he had been able to gain made it clear to him that the struggle with the Crusaders could not be pressed to a conclusion with only the forces of Damascus and those that could be spared from the defence of Egypt. It was not merely that the six thousand troopers whom he could now maintain in the field at one time were insufficient for a decisive campaign. So long as the Nuriya troops at Aleppo were under the control of others, they constituted a potentially hostile force on his flank. But even if they were securely brought over to his side, that very operation would only deepen the hostility of the Zangids of Mosul, who with their six thousand troops would still effectively neutralize him. The conclusion was inescapable; since he could not concentrate the forces of Syria and Egypt against the Crusaders so long as he was endangered by flank or rear attacks from Mosul, the forces of Mosul too must be brought under his control, and turned into auxiliaries in the Holy War.

Having arrived at this conclusion, he set himself to accomplish it. That it could not be done without armed conflict

---

1. *Al Fath al-Qussi*, ed. Landberg, 96–7.
2. After the battle of Marj 'Uyun and again after Taqi ad-Din's campaign against Qilij Arslan, dispatches were sent to Mujahid ad-Din Qaymaz at Mosul: 'Imad, *Barq*, III, ff. 132–5, 138–9.

must have been clear to him, and he was reluctant to take arms against those who were to be his future allies. Persuasion and diplomacy would yield better returns than conquest, and he knew himself to possess one powerful advantage. In the eyes of all Islam he had established his claim to the spiritual succession of Nur ad-Din, and those moral forces that had been fanned into life by Nur ad-Din were ranging themselves on his side.[1] However much the interests of the Zangids might be supported by the narrower loyalties of local patriotism and military tradition, he gained the sympathies of an increasingly influential faction, not only at Aleppo, but also at Mosul.[2]

The rivalries and secret or overt communications of the Zangids with the Franks undermined their own cause, and it seems even that the doctrine of legal rights, so industriously

---

1. The most striking evidence is to be found in the steady drift of the leading '*ulama*' and influential personalities towards his side. Nur ad-Din's two most respected qadis, Diya' ad-Din Shahrazuri and Sharaf ad-Din Ibn Abi 'Asrun, had joined him from the first; indeed, the latter left Aleppo to take up the Qadiship at Damascus as early as 1175 or 1176, thereby, as al-Fadil reminded Saladin in a later letter ('Imad, *Barq*, III, f. 107b), greatly weakening the cause of his adversaries. Cf also Ibn Jubair's account of the public prayers at Mecca in 1183, when at the mention of Saladin's name the whole concourse uttered fervent *Amens* (ed. G.M.S., 97, 3–4) and the course of the negotiations with the Shaikh ash-Shuyukh related below.

2. The fact is obvious from the ultimate surrender of these cities, but the details are very obscure. From his later actions, the leader of the party at Aleppo favourable to Saladin seems to have been Husam ad-Din Tuman. At Mosul (where Ibn al-Athir himself expressly confirms the existence of a pro-Saladin party amongst the amirs, see p. 17, n. 4, above) Saladin would appear at first to have had hopes of gaining the support of the generalissimo Mujahid ad-Din Qaymaz. Although Qaymaz directed the defence of Mosul against Saladin in 578/1182, his dismissal by 'Izz ad-Din in the following year was immediately followed by the adhesion of his two fiefs of Irbil and Jazirat ibn 'Umar to Saladin (Ibn al-Athir, XI, 329; Baha', Schultens, 57 = Cairo, 52) but the precise significance of these two events cannot be determined. According to Ibn al-Athir, XI, 297, Qaymaz had come to power in Mosul by overthrowing the young *wazir* Jalal ad-Din b. Jamal ad-Din, who was suspected of being on friendly terms with Saladin.

pursued by Saladin, helped to turn the scale. He had only to repeat the tactics employed by Nur ad-Din himself against Damascus: to weaken the opposing party by encouraging defections and by organizing military demonstrations at appropriate moments, at the same time observing to the letter his treaty obligations and the sovereign rights of the Caliphate.

Saladin's history during the next six years, 1179 to 1185, is the record of his successive advances towards this aim. The complex tale of compaigns and negotiations with the minor princes of Mesopotamia, the Zangids of Mosul, and the envoys of the Caliphate, though not difficult to unravel, is difficult to present without entering into a mass of detail. With this main thread in the narrative, two others are interwoven: the continued warfare with Jerusalem, and the problems of internal administration and relations between his relatives and vassals. For the sake of clarity, we shall deal with these aspects separately.

During the campaigns of 1179, the Seljuq sultan of Rum, Qilij Arslan, who had in the previous year sent an envoy to assure Saladin of his friendship,[1] suddenly demanded the cession of Ra'ban, captured by Saladin in 1176 from as-Salih.

Taqi ad-Din, in whose command it lay, was dispatched to defend it, and by a stratagem routed the Seljuq forces with his small force of one thousand horsemen.[2] Early in 1180 a quarrel

---

1. 'Imad, dispatch cited in *Barq*, III, f. 123a. The envoy was instructed to inform Saladin that Qilij Arslan was proceeding to Malatya 'to organize its affairs' and expected Saladin either to remain neutral or to support him. Saladin's answer was a forthright statement that 'he would not permit mutual warfare between Muslim princes instead of uniting in the *jihad*, and that this own friendship or hostility depended upon their attitude towards the cause of God'. وهيهات إذ نترك المسلمين يقصد بعضهم بعضاً أو نرى أحداً منهم إلا في سبيل الله وداً أو بغضاً.

2. Abu Shama, II, 9 from 'Imad, *Barq*, III, ff. 137b–138a, and Ibn Abi Tayyi'. The former gives the strength of Qilij Arslan's forces as twenty thousand (the dispatch to Mujahid ad-Din, *Barq*, f. 139a, increases the figure to =

broke out on a domestic issue between the Seljuq sultan and the Artuqid prince of Hisn Kaifa, Nur ad-Din. Although the latter was a vassal of Mosul, he appealed to Saladin, presumably in virtue of the Aleppo treaty of 1176. This was precisely the kind of occasion for which Saladin was waiting. In order to establish his control over Mosul, the first and necessary step was to detach the great vassals of Mesopotamia and Diyar Bakr, who furnished more than half of the effective forces of the Mosul army. The most powerful of these were the Artuqid princes of Hisn Kaifa and Mardi, who had never submitted with grace to the domination of the Zangids. Already in 1178 they had approached Saladin, to obtain his support against the aggressive designs of the Seljuq sultan,[1] and dubious as the present *casus belli* was, he was impelled to seize the opportunity in order to gain their interest and display *de facto* suzerainty over Diyar Bakr. A truce signed with Baldwin in the spring[2] left him free to lead his army to the borders of the Seljuq dominions, less for the purpose of military operations than to force Qilij Arslan to cease these provocations and accept his mediation.[3] The plan achieved even greater success than he could have anticipated. The two sultans met on the Geuk Su in June and there, apparently, concluded the

---

= thirty thousand) whereas Ibn Abi Tayyi' gives the more reasonable figure of thirty thousand horsemen. Ibn al-Athir, XI, 305, is based on 'Imad ad-Din, even as to the figures, which he quotes with a *yuqalu*.

1. 'Imad, *Barq*, III, f. 123a: فإن ملوك ديار بكر إلينا مرتجون ولنا ملتجون ويحبلنا معتصمون... ومن سلطان الروم مستشعرون ويسلطاننا مستنصرون... ولتلينا نداهم وقوّينا رجاهم.

2. Baha' (Schultens, 47 = Cairo, 43) asserts that the '*askar* of Aleppo accompanied Saladin on this expedition, but his narrative is open to question on several points. The truce is mentioned by 'Imad *apud* Abu Shama, II, 16 (Ibn al-Athir, XI, 307) and William of Tyre, XXII, 1 (trans., II, 447), who describes its terms as 'somewhat humiliating to us'.

3. *Michel le syrien*, III, 388, asserts that on Saladin's advance Qilij Arslan destroyed the wall of Kaisun and deported the inhabitants, and that after the junction of Saladin and Nur ad-Din on the river Sanga, peace was arranged by the mediation of an envoy from Qilij Arslan, named Hassan.

alliance that was to mean so much to Saladin in later years. Its first fruits were a short and successful campaign against Ruben of Little Armenia, on the pretext of harsh treatment of the Turkmen tribes in his territories.

Baha' ad-Din relates that on the conclusion of this campaign a general peace was concluded, on the initiative of Qilij Arslan, between Saladin, the Seljuq sultan, Mosul, and the princes of Diyar Bakr at a meeting on the river Sanja, near Sumaisat, on 2 October 1180. There is no confirmation of this statement in any other contemporary source, and indeed the evidence is all against it. For on 29 June Saif ad-Din of Mosul had died and his brother 'Izz ad-Din, setting aside Saif ad-Din's nomination of his son Sanjarshah, had succeeded him. On his accession 'Izz ad-Din sent an envoy to Saladin to ask his agreement to the continuance of the suzerainty of Mosul over the Mesopotamian cities seized by Saif ad-Din after Nur ad-Din's death in 1174. Saladin refused point-blank. These provinces, he said, were included in the general grant made to him by the caliph, and he had left them in Saif ad-Din's possession only in return for his promise to assist Saladin with his troops. At the same time, he sent a dispatch to Baghdad, pointing out that he could not draw indefinitely on the Egyptian forces for his Syrian campaigns but needed the armies of those provinces, and asking for a confirmation of the grant, which was sent to him accordingly.[1]

The breach with Mosul was consummated by the death of as-Salih at Aleppo on 4 December 1181. Saladin was in Egypt at the time, and on learning of as-Salih's illness had sent urgent orders to Taqi ad-Din at Hamah and Farrukshah at Damascus to occupy the western Jazira and prevent the army of Mosul from crossing the Euphrates. But Farrukshah was engaged in

---

1. 'Imad, *apud* Abu Shama, II, 17.

countering Reynald's scheme of invading Arabia from Karak, and Taqi ad-Din was unable to prevent 'Izz ad-Din from entering Aleppo.[1] The confusion that had followed as-Salih's death was ended by 'Izz ad-Din's appointment of his own brother 'Imad ad-Din as governor of the city, in exchange for Sinjar, and after emptying the contents of its treasury and arsenal he returned to Mosul.[2] Saladin's intense anxiety over the situation is shown by the succession of letters addressed to the caliph's *diwan*, contrasting the conduct of the prince of Mosul in seizing a province that had been assigned to him, while his troops were in the very act of protecting the city of the Prophet (Madina) from the infidel, complaining that the disputes between the Muslim princes were hindering the *jihad*, reasserting his claim to Aleppo on the basis of his diploma from the Caliphate, and declaring that 'if the Exalted Commands should ordain that the prince of Mosul be invested with the government of Aleppo, then it was better to invest him with all Syria and Egypt as well'.[3] The urgent tone of these letters is no doubt explained partly by the necessity to counteract the similar pressure of the partisans of Mosul at Baghdad, but though propaganda points may be difficult to disentangle from religious zeal, there can be little doubt that Saladin was genuinely in

---

1. Dispatches quoted by Abu Shama, II, 22–3. Ibn al-Athir, XI, 312, 315, relates that there was a rising at Hamah, and that Taqi ad-Din was forced to 'flee' back to Hamah from Manbij. In the absence of confirmation his statements must be treated with suspicion.

2. Abu Shama, II, 22 (quoting Baha', Schultens, 48 = Cairo, 44–5). The latter (who was still at the time a *qadi* in Mosul) adds that his troops refused to face the campaigns against Saladin which the occupation of Aleppo would entail, and that the generalissimo Mujahid ad-Din Qaymaz 'could not stomach the rudeness of the Syrian amirs'. On the confused situation at Aleppo before 'Imad ad-Din's establishment, see C. Cahen, *La Syrie du nord a l'époque des croisades*, Paris, 1940, p. 421.

3. Dispatches quoted by Abu Shama, II, 23.

earnest over the stalemate that would follow from a reunion of Mosul and Aleppo.

In May 1182 he left Cairo, accompanied by half of the newly reorganized regular army of Egypt, some five thousand troopers in all,[1] and rejoined his lieutenants in Syria. After an unsuccessful *coup de main* against Beirut by sea and land, he marched with his Egyptian forces on Aleppo, fortified in his purpose by the caliph's diploma.[2] But before investing it, he was visited by MuZaffar ad-Din Geukburi, the governor of Harran, with an urgent invitation to cross the Euphrates and assurances that he would be welcomed on all sides.[3] Accordingly, since he

---

1. 'Imad, *apud* Abu Shama, II, 27 (the first five pages of the MS. of vol. V of *Barq* (Bodl. Marsh. 425) are missing). Al-Maqrizi, *Khitat*, I, 86 (ed. Wiet, II, 1, 17), preserves a report from the diary of al-Fadil on the reorganization of the Egyptian *askar* in Rajab 577 (November 1181), giving the total numbers as 111 amirs, 6,976 *tawashis* or regular mamluks, and 1,553 *qaraghulams*, i.e., 8,640 in all, exclusive of unbeneficed (*mahlulun*, i.e., free) troopers, Arabs, and the remains of the Fatimid regiments. In a brief and incomplete note by Ibn Mammati (p. 369), the pay and allowances for each category of troops are listed on the basis of the assessed value (*'ibra*, the money account being the *dinar jundi*.

2. Ibn al-Athir, XI, 317, asserts that the march on Aleppo was a feint, and to give substance to his statement, represents Geukburi as having made his proposition to Saladin during the attack on Beirut. But 'Imad (*Barq*, f. 5b) says definitely that Saladin intended to attack Aleppo and (ibid., 8b) speaks of Geukburi's envoy arriving unexpectedly *wa-ma sha'arna illa birasuli Muzaffar ad-Din* to propose the change of plan after the halt before Aleppo, subsequently reinforced by the arrival of Geukburi himself. That Saladin had in fact received the diploma for Aleppo is clear from al-Fadil's letter to the *diwan* after its capture, which opens with the words 'This homage is sent after he has received the surrender of the city of Aleppo, in obedience to the command issued to him' ('Imad, *Barq*, V, f. 93b: صدرت هـذه الخدمة وقد تسلم مدينة حلب ممتثلاً للأمر الوارد عليه واقفاً حيث وقف به الاختيار له).

3. 'Imad, *Barq*, V, ff. 8b–9a, *Michel le syrien*, III, 389, also attributes the initiative to Geukburi, and mentions the dispersal of the forces of Mosul and its vassals on Saladin's advance. Ibn Abi Tayyi' (*apud* Abu Shama, II, 30) asserts that Geukberi (who had formerly commanded the armies of Mosul) had been *shihna* of Aleppo and tried to seize the citadel, but was foiled and given Harran instead by 'Izz ad-Din when the latter made the exchange =

was in fact, by virtue of the caliph's diploma, lawful ruler of the Euphrates and Khabur provinces, Saladin crossed the Euphrates at the end of September and with only scattered opposition occupied the former possession of the atabeg Nur ad-Din in the Jazira.[1] 'Izz ad-Din attempted to take the field against him, but was foiled by the opposition of his own officers and the open

---

=   with 'Imad ad-Din. Kamal ad-Din (Blochet, 72–3) asserts that 'Imad ad-Din himself proposed to Saladin that he should capture Sinjar and give it back to him in exchange for Aleppo. But although some years earlier 'Imad ad-Din had appealed to Saladin when Saif ad-Din besieged him in Sinjar (see p. 22, n. 3 above), there is nothing in the very detailed narrative of the secretary 'Imad to support the story, which is most probably an anticipation of the arrangement made on the surrender of Aleppo. It may well, however, have been in Saladin's mind.

1. Saladin crossed at al-Bira, whose governor had appealed to him earlier in the year for assistance against the aggression of the Artuqid prince of Mardin at the instigation of 'Izz ad-Din (Ibn al-Athir, XI, 313–14). Saruj surrendered and its governor, Ibn Malik, was confirmed in possession. At Edessa the governor az-Za'farani resisted, but after a siege of three days surrendered and the city was given to Geukburi. Ibn al-Athir's statement (ibid., 318) that 'Izz ad-Din sent forces to defend Edessa is not supported by other sources, but the fact of the siege (not mentioned by Abu Shama) is confirmed by 'Imad, *Barq*, V, f. 20a. Raqqa was held by Saladin's old rival Yanal al-Manbiji, who joined 'Izz ad-Din, and the town was given to the former governor of Edessa, az-Za'farani. The Khabur province was rapidly overrun and was given to the Kurdish general Jamal ad-Din Khushtarin (on whom, see Ibn Abi Tayyi', *apud* Abu Shama, I, 167 foot. He had distinguished himself at the battle of Marj 'Uyun by taking Baldwin, son of Balian, prisoner: 'Imad, *Barq*, III, 130b–131a). The citadel at Nasibin also held out for a few days, and another Kurd, Husam ad-Din Abu'l-Haija', was installed as governor, but subsequently removed for his oppressive conduct ('Imad, *apud* Abu Shama, II, 33). With his usual liberality the campaign proved almost too successful for Saladin's financial resources, and he was forced to send urgent requests for money to Farrukhshah, and al-'Adil: 'Every time a city opens its gates, desires open their mouths; the treasuries are exhausted by expenditure and donations, and we have entered a sea which nothing will bar but another sea' (Abu Shama, II, 30, from 'Imad, *Barq*, V, ff. 19–22, 13 (the folios are in disorder)). The whole campaign, down to the action of Nur ad-Din b. Qara Arslan in joining Saladin and the appeal of the ruler of Mosul to the princes of Azerbaijan and Northern Persia, is strikingly reminiscent of Nur ad-Din's own campaign against Mosul in 566/1170: Ibn. al-Athir, XI, 238–9.

adhesion to Saladin of his chief vassal, the Artuqid prince of Hisn Kaifa, Nur ad-Din ibn Qara Arslan.[1] The sole result of his action was to supply Saladin with a valid reason for advancing on Mosul itself, an action justified by him in a lengthy dispatch to Baghdad, accusing the rulers of Mosul of paying the Franks to attack him, of oppression of their subjects, and finally of appealing to the sworn enemy of the Caliphate, the Seljuq *atabeg* in Persia.[2] The last accusation is confirmed by the Mosul sources; in desperation 'Izz ad-Din was seeking help in every direction and sent Baha' ad-Din himself to ask for the caliph's support against Saladin.[3] In response to this appeal, the caliph sent a delegate to mediate between the parties, and for a month protacted negotiations went on, while Saladin's nephew Taqi ad-Din and brother Taj al-Muluk continued to prosecute the siege.[4]

It must be emphasized that the point at issue in these

---

1. 'Imad, *Barq*, V, 19a (Abu Shama, II, 32), relates that the prince Nur ad-Din's envoy reached Saladin at Bira, and undertook on his behalf to give loyal service if Saladin would promise to obtain Amid for him.
2. Abu Shama, II, 31–2. The *atabeg* was Jahan-Pahlawan b. Ildeghiz, who regarded himself as regent for the Seljuq sultan Turghril b. Arslanshah. On the relations of these princes with the Caliphate, see Barthold, *Turkestan down to the Mongul Invasion*, repr., London, 1958, 346–7; C. E. Bosworth, 'The Iranian World (A. D. 1000–1217)'; in *The Cambridge History of Iran*, V, 169–70.
3. Baha', Schultens, 50 = Cairo, 46. He adds that Jahan-Pahlawan replied by an offer to help on conditions 'which were more perilous even than fighting Saladin', i.e., the recognition of the suzerainty of Sultan Tughril.
4. 'Imad (*Barq*, V, 15a, and in his dispatch to the *diwan*, ibid., 23a) says that in response to the shaikh's appeals, Saladin stopped active operations during the negotiations, but does not imply that the siege was lifted. He encamped before Mosul on 11 Rajab (10 November) and left about 12 Sha'ban (11 December). The Shaikh ash-Shuyukh was 'Abd al-Rahim b. Isma'il b. Ahmad al-Naisaburi, the son of a celebrated Shafi'i scholar known as Abu Sa'd b. Abi Salih, see Subki, *Tabaqat al Shafi'iya*, IV, 204. Saladin had been in correspondence with him for some years; a dispatch addressed to him in 575 AH ('Imad, *Barq*, III, 134a–136a) on the exploits of the Egyptian fleet in the Red Sea, opens with an apology for an intermission in the correspondence.

negotiations was not at any time Saladin's claim to the physical possession of Mosul, but the terms on which the prince of Mosul would adhere to Saladin and send his armies to cooperate in the war with the Franks. On this first occasion the main object of the Zangid prince was to retain his suzerainty over Aleppo, and although Saladin, anxious to reach an agreement, yielded to all his demands short of this, he refused to ratify the terms. At the urgent intercession of the shaikh, Saladin agreed to withdraw from Mosul, but refused to continue the negotiations.[1] The fact that they were set on foot had severely strained the confidence of his new vassals in the Jazira and, in order to reassure them, he announced to the *diwan* his firm determination not to leave the province until he had completed the conquest of it.[2]

He began, therefore, by besieging 'Izz ad-Din's brother in Sinjar, with the assistance of Nur ad-Din of Hisn Kaifa. It was surrendered on terms after fifteen days (30 December) and the garrison was evacuated to Mosul.[3] After Dara also had been

---

1. The whole course of the negotiations is narrated at length by 'Imad who was himself one of the negotiators, in *Barq*, V, ff. 11–12, 15–16. According to his account, when the shaikh ash-Shuyukh, after the rejection of the agreement, finally left Mosul in anger at the duplicity of the Mosul authorities, he returned to Saladin and 'told him what he had seen and heard of their divisions'. There is no indication of the roles played by the envoys of Qizil Arslan of Azerbaijan and Shah Arman of Khilat, who also offered to mediate ('Imad, *Barq*, V, f. 26a; Ibn al-Athir, XI, 321). Saladin's refusal to resume negotiations is contained in a later dispatch to Shaikh ash-Shuyukh, 'Imad, *Barq*, V, 33a.

2. 'Imad, *Barq*, V, ff. 12a–b, and dispatch written by 'Imad to the *diwan*, ibid., 23b–24a.

3. A relieving force sent from Mosul towards Sinjar was surprised by Taqi ad-Din at Aranjan and sent back stripped of its equipment ('Imad, *Barq*, V, 17a). Shah Arman again attempted to intercede with Saladin for Sinjar, but refused to accept his terms (ibid., 50b). The capture of the town is attributed by Ibn al-Athir (XI, 321) to the treachery of a Kurdish amir, who admitted the besiegers by night. This story is to some extent confirmed by the implications of 'Imad's account: *Barq*, V, 27b) (not in Abu Shama). ▪

surrendered by its Artuqid prince Bahram, Saladin dismissed his forces and went into winter quarters at Harran with his regiment of guards at the end of February 1183. But that he had no intention of relaxing the pressure upon 'Izz ad-Din is shown by the vigorous correspondence directed to the chief ministers at Baghdad and repeated requests for his recognition as suzerain of Mosul.[1] Though this was still withheld, his application to receive the caliph's diploma for Amid was granted.[2] In April 'Izz ad-Din made a last attempt to rally his remaining allies,[3] but Saladin called up Taqi ad-Din from Hamah and on his approach the coalition was dissolved. Without waiting for the remainder of his forces, he at once laid siege to the all but impregnable fortress of Amid in Diyar Bakr, in pursuance of his promise to Nur ad-Din. Its surrender within three weeks set the seal on his reputation, and his quixotic generosity, both to the defeated governor and in handing it over with its immense stores intact to Nur ad-Din,[4] disproved

---

= Lane-Poole's statement that Sinjar was sacked (*Saladin*, London, 1898, 171) does not appear to be based on any of the firsthand sources. Sinjar was given in fief to Sa'd ad-Din Mas'ud b. Unar, the son of Mu'in ad-Din Unar, the former prince of Damascus, with whom Saladin left a party of his own afficers, ('Imad, *Barq*, V, 31a). Baha's statement (Schultens, 50 = Cairo, 46) that it was given to Taqi ad-Din is erroneous; the actual diploma of Sa'd ad-Din's appointment is reproduced in the *Barq*. It seems clear that Saladin did not give it to any of his relatives or princely vassals, since he wished to hold it in reserve for 'Imad ad-Din of Aleppo (see p.34, n. 2 above). A noteworthy feature of 'Imad's account of the siege is his description of the sobriety and discipline of Saladin's own troops, whom he contrasts with the disorderly Kurds in the Artuqid army (17b).

1. Dispatches from al-Fadil, and 'Imad, to the *diwan* ('Imad, *Barq*, V, ff. 23–4, 34–6) and to the Shaikh ash-Shuyukh (32–3).
2. Dispatch of al-Fadil, 'Imad, *Barq*, V, 53b–54a (Abu Shama, II, 40, ll. 6–7).
3. The armies that assembled at Kharzam (near Mardin) were those of Mosul, of the Shah Arman Sukman of Khilat, Qutb ad-Din Ilghazi b. Albi of Mardin, Dawlatshah of Arzan and Bidlis, and some of the troops of Aleppo; 'Imad, *Barq*, V, 50–2 (Abu Shama, II, 38); dispatch of al-Fadil, 'Imad, *Barq*, V, 53a; Ibn al-Athir, XI, 322.
4. The terms of the oath taken by Nur ad-Din ('Imad, *Barq*, V, 73a) =

once and for all his enemies' imputation of selfish ambition.[1]

In his dispatches to the Caliphate after the capture of Amid Saladin himself pointed the moral. The caliph's authority to take and govern Amid had unlocked its gates to him; why was the patent for Mosul still denied? This alone stood in the way of the union of Islam and the recovery of Jerusalem. Let the commander of the Faithful compare the conduct of his clients and judge which of them had most faithfully served the cause of Islam. If Saladin insists on the inclusion of Mesopotamia and Mosul in his dominions it is because 'this little Jazira i.e., Mesopotamia is the lever which will set in motion the great Jazira i.e., the whole Arab East; it is the point of division and centre of resistance, and once it is set in its place in the chain of alliances, the whole armed might of Islam will be coordinated to engage the forces of unbelief'.[2]

The submission of Amid brought the remaining Artuqids at Mayyafariqin and Mardin over to Saladin,[3] and he now turned

---

= are adequately summarized by Abu Shama (II, 41): that he would govern with justice and put down all oppression, that he would be a loyal subject of the sultan, and enemy of his enemies and a friend of his friends at all times, and that whensoever assistance was requested by Amid to fight against the Franks he would be prompt to answer the call.

1. The whole episode is described in detail and in epic style by 'Imad in *Barq*, V, ff. 49–65, a literary masterpiece which is in no way adequately represented by the bald summary of Abu Shama, II, 39–40. Ibn al-Athir, XI, 324–5, is (as usual) based also on 'Imad, but his attempt to explain away the capture of the fortress by the foolish and grasping conduct of the governor is in direct contradiction to 'Imad's account (f. 60a) and is repeated, with little more justification, three pages later to explain Saladin's capture of Aleppo.

2. 'Imad, *Barq*, V, 69a–71a and 68, Abu Shama, II, 40–1.

3. 'Imad (*Barq*, V, 75–6; Abu Shama, II, 42) relates with great gusto how he spent the night writing out their patents of appointment. The governor of Mayyafariqin was made a sub-vassal owing allegiance to Nur ad-Din ('Imad, *Barq*, 76b), but the prince of Mardin, Qutb, ad-Din, remained a direct vassal (77a). *Michel le syrien*, III, 394, says that Saladin, after much fighting, eventually purchased Mayyafariqin but in its context this notice appears to belong to the campaign of 1185.

back to settle his account with Aleppo, receiving on the way the submission of the last outer fortresses of the city, Tall Khalid and 'Ain Tab.[1] By 21 May he was already encamped before Aleppo, with a reasonable expectation of its early surrender.[2] Nevertheless, Nur ad-Din's old guard fought against him with as much determination as ever. Saladin's secretary vividly presents the strange complexity of the conflict; neither 'Imad ad-Din Zangi nor Saladin was eager to fight, the former because he had set his heart on returning to Sinjar, the latter because the Nuriya, the *atabeg* Nur ad-Din's old guard, were 'the soldiers of the *jihad*, who had in the past done great services for Islam' and 'whose gallantry and courage had gained his admiration', whereas they for their part 'stirred up the flames of war' and the younger and more ardent of Saladin's own troops, notwithstanding his admonitions and those of his more experienced officers, plunged eagerly into the fray, headed by his brother Taj al-Muluk who was killed in the battle.[3] After a

---

1. Tall Khalid was assigned to Basr ad-Din Dildirim b. Baha' ad-Dawla b. Yaruq, the governor of Tall Bashir, 'in recognition of his promptitude in giving allegiance', its castle being destroyed; 'Ain Tab remained in the possession of its governor Nasih ad-Din Muhammad b. Khumartagin: 'Imad, *Barq*, V, 99 (Abu Shama, II, 42).

2. The change of attitude of the citizens is indicated by the report of Kamal ad-Din (III, 63; Blochet, 76) that 'Imad ad-Din thought it advisable to take hostages from them, 'for fear that they might surrender the city to Saladin'. It is difficult to understand the reasons for which Imad ad-Din in the preceding year had taken the step of destroying the citadels guarding the eastern approaches to Aleppo (ibid., III, 59, Blochet, 74–5).

3. 'Imad, *Barq*, V, ff. 79–83. Kamal ad-Din's account (III, 63–7) tallies in essentials with that of Imad, but he has taken some details from Ibn al-Athir, notably the story of 'Imad ad-Din's interview with his armies. Blochet has evidently misunderstood this passage, which, however, seems to have its origin in the secretary 'Imad's statement that 'he was set on putting an end to the conflict ... and found that he was paying out 30,000 dinars a month to the troops and that if the siege were prolonged without hope of success, he would become bankrupt' (راح الربح ورسخ الخسار) ('Imad, *Barq*, f. 84b). It was at this juncture that he arranged to send the amir Tuman al-Yaruqi secretly =

few days he withdrew to the hill of Jawshan, overlooking the city, set his builders to construct a fortress there, and started to distribute the territories of Aleppo in fief to his own troops. 'Imad ad-Din Zangi saw that the critical moment had come, and secretly arranged the exchange of Aleppo for Sinjar and the eastern Jazira, on condition of his cooperation in the war with the Franks. On 11 June, Saladin's yellow banner was hoisted on the citadel, although he himself did not accupy it until 'Imad ad-Din had removed all his treasure, and secured possession of his new provinces. The Nuriya troops in turn made their submission with what, from the external events, would seem surprising readiness, were received by Saladin as old comrades in arms, and overwhelmed by his generosity. The governor of Harim alone held out and attempted to assure himself of support from Antioch, but was arrested by his own men, who surrendered the castle to Saladin in person on 22 June.[1]

A truce with Bohemond of Antioch having been arranged on condition of the liberation of Muslim prisoners, Saladin was now in a position to retaliate on the Franks of Jerusalem for their raiding expeditions during his absence in Mesopotamia, and more especially on Reynald at Karak for his forays in Arabia and on the Red Sea. Announcing to the *diwan* at Baghdad his decision to prosecute the *jihad*, now that the main obstacles had been removed,[2] he set out with the regular troops of Aleppo

---

= as his emissary to Saladin 'with whom the amir was on terms of friendship from of old'. The joy of victory was dimmed for Saladin by the death from wounds of his brother Taj al-Muluk Buri ('Imad, *Barq*, f. 96b), a circumstance that was dramatically worked up by Ibn al-Athir (XI, 328) with the dubious addition that he had intended to appoint Taj al-Muluk as governor of Aleppo.

1. 'Imad's dispatch ('Imad, *Barq*, V, 89b–90a; Abu Shama, II, 48) says only that the troops at Harim suspected the governor Surkhak of correspondence with the Franks and sent him as a prisoner to Aleppo. Saladin appointed Ibrahim b. Shuruh as governor in his place.

2. Dispatches of al-Fadil ('Imad, *Barq*, V, 94a; Abu Shama, II, 48 inf.) and 'Imad (*Barq*, 108a).

and the Jazira, together with the Turkmen cavalry and a large force of volunteers and auxiliaries.[1] After a brief halt at Damascus, he crossed the Jordan to Baisan on 29 September, but failed to bring the main forces of the kingdom to battle.[2] Returning to Damascus, he summoned al-'Adil to join him before Karak with a body of the Egyptian troops, and laid siege to the castle in November. The Muslim forces were so confident of success that the failure of their mangonels to effect a breach produced a corresponding discouragement, and when news was received of the arrival of a relieving force at Wala, they found excuses for putting off the attack and Saladin withdrew to rest and refit his armies.[3]

During the interval before the attack, another attempt was made to solve the problem of Mosul by negotiation. The initiative came from 'Izz ad-Din, who had imprudently arrested his generalissimo Mujahid ad-Din, with the result that his own nephew Sanjarshah, at Jazirat ibn 'Umar, with Geukburi's brother at Irbil and the governors Takrit and Haditha, threw themselves on the protection of Saladin and through envoys obtained from him a guarantee of support.[4] 'Izz ad-Din

---

1. 'Imad, *Barq*, V, 108b–109a.
2. The principal account is given in a lengthy dispatch reproduced in 'Imad, *Barq*, V, ff. 112a–114a, from which Abu Shama's narrative (II, 50) is derived by skillful but ruthless pruning. A second dispatch in very similar terms follows in 'Imad, *Barq*, ff. 114b–116b.
3. Detailed narrative in 'Imad, *Barq*, V, 118a–119a and 126b, Abu Shama, II, 51.
4. 'Imad *apud* Abu Shama, II, 53, from 'Imad, *Barq*, V, f. 130. Sanjarshah had been nominated by his father Saif ad-Din to succeed him at Mosul but was removed by 'Izz ad-Din and compensated by the government of Jazirat ibn 'Umar under the conrtol of Mujahid ad-Din Qaymaz. As his fief is commonly called *al-Jazira* by the Arabic writers, Western historians have confused it at times with Mesopotamia. It is an interesting commentary on the attitude towards Mosul in Baghdad that, according to Ibn al-Athir, XI, 329, the caliph an-Nasir had taken advantage of the same incident to seize Duquq. Ibn Abi Tayyi' *apud* Abu Shama, II, 53, speaks of envoys also from al-Pahlawan, Qizil Arslan and Shah Arman, but this is unlikely in itself and there is no reference to their presence in the direct sources.

appealed to the caliph to send the Shaikh ash-Shuyukh once more to mediate with Saladin, 'knowing', as Saladin's secretary wrote, 'that our policy was one of strict obedience to the caliph's commands.'[1] An agreement was reached with the shaikh on the basis that 'Izz ad-Din's rights in Mosul would be respected, and that his former vassals should be left free to choose between Saladin and him, but it was rejected by the envoy from Mosul, and so matters remained as they were, or rather worse.[2]

For his fresh assault on Karak (August–September 1184) Saladin assembled the most powerful army that had yet operated in Syria, comprising the forces of Damascus, Aleppo, the Jazira and Sinjar, Hisn Kaifa and Mardin, and a contingent from Egypt. Again it failed, and the armies were dismissed after a raiding expedition through Samaria. Back at Damascus, he found the shaikh awaiting him with the caliph's patents for his new provinces and official robes for his chief vassals as well as for himself.[3] This was followed by graver news. 'Izz ad-Din of

---

1. 'Imad, *Barq*, V, f. 129a. لعلمهم أنا لا نرى إلا الاعتماد بالطاعة للأمر المطاع.
2. By a rare coincidence these negotiations are reported by two writers who took a leading part in them on both sides. Baha' accompanied the chief *qadi* of Mosul, Muhyi ad-Din al-Shahrazuri (Schultens, 57 = Cairo, 52) and his account fully agrees with that of 'Imad (*Baraq*, V ff. 127a–132b) on the general conduct and outcome of the negotiations, as against the misleading statement of Ibn al-Athir, XI, 330. 'Imad's narrative is detailed and lively, particularly in his desciption of the overbearing attitude of Muhyi ad-Din. Saladin was anxious to reach an agreement, and even after Muhyi ad-Din's rejection of the formula approved by the Shaikh ash-Shuyukh made a last effort to prevent a breakdown. But the *qadi* refused outright to reopen discussions and by his violence and threats only succeeded in convincing Saladin, who had been 'reluctant to return to Mosul' that there was no alternative (132b: وكان السلطان فاتر العزم في العود إلى الموصل فهاجه وحرف إليها مزاجه). 'Imad mentions also that he was related by marriage to the Shaikh ash-Shuyukh, whose wife was the daughter of his uncle, the former *wazir* Abu Nasr Ahmad b. Hamid (*Barq*, 128a). The extant portions of *al-Barq al-Shami* end, unfortunately, with this episode and the notification to 'Imad ad-Din of Sinjar and to Taqi ad-Din of Saladin's intention to resume the attack of Karak.
3. 'Imad, *apud* Abu Shama, II, 56, 60; Baha', Schultens, 59 = Cairo, 54. =

Mosul had accepted the offers of the *atabeg* of Persia, and had received a reinforcement of three thousand horsemen from the *atabeg* Qilij Arslan of Azerbaijan for an attack on Irbil. Although the attack was unsuccessful, the governor called on Saladin to honour his promise, and thus provided the occasion for Saladin's renewed assault on Mosul.[1]

Before setting out in the following year, however, he had the good fortune to be invited by Raymond of Tripoli to agree to a truce for four years.[2] With his rear thus protected, he assembled his forces at Aleppo in May 1185, crossed the Euphrates, and marched on Mosul, although he had been warned by the Seljuq sultan Qilij Arslan that he would be opposed by a coalition of the 'eastern princes'.[3] But Mosul was in fact left to its fate, and

---

= The robes were sent for al-'Adil, Nasir ad-Din b. Shirkuh, and Nur ad-Din of Hisn Kaifa. Abu Shama quotes also the terms of Saladin's diploma conferring Irbil on Zain ad-Din Yusuf b. 'Ali Kuchak, which laid stress, as usual, on the obligations of engaging in the *jihad*. The territories comprised in the diploma were Irbil with its citadel and dependencies, the whole region of the Great Zab, Shahrizur and its dependencies, the ranges (*ma'ayish*) of the House of Qipchaq (Turkmen) and of Qarabli, ed-Dast, and the Zarzariya (Kurds). On the widespread Turkmen-Kurd feud which broke out in 1185 and lasted for eight years, see *Michel le syrien*, III, 400–42 (a clear account, giving many precise details).

1. 'Imad and Baha', loc. cit., Ibn al-Athir, XI, 332. Ibn al-Athir stigmatizes the violence and brutality of the Persian troops of Azerbaijan, and describes the revulsion with which Mujahid ad-Din observed the conduct of his new allies. Although he draws no conclusions, it is very possible that this was a factor in the submission of Mosul to Saladin in the following year. In *Atabegs* (R.H.C., Or., II, 2, 335–6) Ibn al-Athir relates a siege of Sanjarshah by 'Izz ad-Din in Rabi', I, 581 – i.e., at the precise date when Sanjarshah was accompanying Saladin in his advance on Mosul. The story is revised in his *Kamil* (XII, 38–40) dated 587, and the occasion referred to Saladin's instructions to 'Izz ad-Din.

2. See p. 48, n. 2 below.

3. On crossing the Euphrates Saladin took a step which it is not easy to interpret with certainty. Geukburi's envoys had undertaken that on Saladin's arrival at Harran Geukburi would 'make up his arears, meet all the requirements in the way of supplies and expenses in that province, and =

even the caliph now refused to intervence further, presumably because (as Saladin lost no opportunity of reminding him) 'Izz ad-Din had been forced to acknowledge the sultan Tughril as his suzerain.[1] During the summer heats Saladin slackened off the siege, and leaving part of his forces in front of Mosul, led the rest northwards to deal with a confused situation that had arisen there after the deaths of Nur ad-Din and the princes of Khilat and Mardin. Before leaving, he applied to the caliph for formal investiture with the sovereignty of Armenia, Diyar Bakr and Mosul, and received in reply the patent for 'the supervision of Diyar Bakr and the interests of its orphan princes'. With or without this, he succeeded in restoring his position in Mayyafariqin, Mardin and Amid, although Pahlawan forestalled him at Khilat.[2]

= pay a sum of 50,000 dinars'. The engagement was not kept, whereupon Saladin, fearing that he might be turning disloyal, dispossessed him of the citadels of Harran and Edessa and kept him under observation. But, later on, convinced that Geukburi was really trustworthy, he restored the citadels to him ('Imad, *apud* Abu Shama, II, 61; Baha', Schultens, 60 = Cairo, 54–5). Ibn al-Athir (XI, 331) represents his release of Geukburi as due to fear of popular disaffection, implying that Saladin had really intended to remove him from his fiefs altogether. But it is hard to understand why, if Saladin really did not trust Geukburi, he should have singled him out shortly afterwards for the distinction of marrying his sister, Rabi'a Khatun, after the death of her first husband Mas'ud b. Unar in September 1185 ('Imad, *apud* Abu Shaa, II, 67, who adds that she died in 643 AH, the last survivor of the children of Ayyub).

1. Baha', Schultens, 62 = Cairo, 56; he was himself the envoy sent to Baghdad, and adds that Pahlawan also refused to send assistance. For Saladin's mission to the caliph, 'Imad, *apud* Abu Shama, II, 62.

2. Mardin was governed by an amir, Nizam ad-Din b. Albqush on behalf of the minor son of Qutb ad-Din, and another of his amirs, Asad ad-Din Yariqtash (?), had occupied Mayyafariqin, and held out against Saladin until an accommodation was reached through Qutb ad-Din's widow. On the death of Nur ad-Din b. Qara Arslan on 15 July 1185, he was succeeded by his son Qutb ad-Dun Sukman; but 'Imad ad-Din b. Qara Arslan, who commanded his brother Nur ad-Din's forces before Mosul, attempted to seize Amid for himself. Failing in this, he seized Khartbirt instead. Before returning =

Returning to Mosul in November, he prepared to continue the siege through the winter. In a last attempt to stave off the now inevitable end, 'Izz ad-Din appealed to Saladin's chivalry by sending out a delegation of the Zangid princesses to intercede.[1] But the issue at stake was too serious, and Saladin could promise no more than to accept the mediation of 'Imad ad-Din Zangi of Sinjar. What followed is not quite clear. Saladin suddenly fell ill, and 'repenting of his rebuff to the envoys, sent to 'Imad ad-Din to dispatch a mission to Mosul'. Without waiting for the conclusion of the negotiations he left Mosul on 25 December for Harran and withdrew his troops to Nasibin. In the following February 'Izz ad-Din, having already been forced to concede to Saladin possession of the territories of his allies south of the Greater Zab, including Irbil and Shahrizur, sent the *qadi* Baha' ad-Din as his envoy to Harran with instructions to get a sworn agreement on the best terms that he could. Saladin restored to him the small district of Bain an-Nahrain, lying between Nasibin and the Tigris, and on swearing to these conditions was recognized as suzerain of Mosul, and 'Izz ad-Din undertook to send his troops to support him in the

---

= to Mosul, Saladin left his trusted mamluk Husam ad-Din Sunqur al-Khilati in command of Diyar Bakr. *Michel le syrien*, II, 397, mentions the seizure of Shabakhtan by the governor of Edessa from Mardin on Saladin's orders, and an unsuccessful attack by the troops of Mardin on Edessa; after which Saladin advanced on Mardin, but 'being uable to capture it by flattering promises', he accepted the ruler of Mardin as a direct vassal.

1. Ibn al-Athir, XI, 337, places this incident at the beginning of the siege, and attempts to deny that it was an indication of the weakness of 'Izz ad-Din's position. But 'Imad (Abu Shama, II, 64) places it, more credibly, after Saladin's return from Mayyafariqin. That it was, in fact, a desperate expedient is shown by the similar action of Ibn Nisan during the siege of Amid (see Abu Shama, II, 40). A typical example of pseudo-historical 'reconciliation' is given by Abu'l-Faraj Barhebraeus in his *Syriac Chronography* (tr. Budge, London, 1932, 319) where, drawing upon both 'Imad ad-Din and Ibn al-Athir, he combines the two narratives and on Saladin's return says 'the mem of Mosul sent those same women a second time to supplicate for peace'.

reconquest of Palestine.[1] The grand coalition was formed at
last.

Throughout all these years, in which Saladin was devoting his
chief attention to organizing the forces for the coming struggle, it
was clearly to his advantage to avoid any major operations
against the Franks. In 1180, after the defeats inflicted on them
during the previous year, and in view of the shortage of supplies
due to a succession of years of drought, he had willingly agreed
to a truce with Baldwin on both land and sea. Raymond of
Tripoli had, it seems, refused to become a consenting party, and
was only brought to reason by a series of devastating raids as
well as the seizure of Aradus by the Egyptian fleet.[2] One of the
most important stipulations from Saladin's point of view was the
freedom of trade, since the route between Egypt and Damascus,
lying as it did between the Crusading castles in the coastal
province and the outposts of Karak and Shawbak, was
precariously exposed and in times of warfare caravans had to be
convoyed by bodies of troops. It was the violation of this
condition by Reynald of Karak in 1182 that gave the signal for
the reopening of hostilities. Already in the autumn of 1181 he
had made a raid on Taima, in the northern Hijaz, from which he

---

1. 'Imad, *apud* Abu Shama, II, 64, and Baha', Schultens, 62 = Cairo, 56–7. Ibn
   al-Athir (XI, 337–41) gives, as usual, a certain amount of imaginative detail,
   but adds the significant statements that there was a party among the amirs at
   Mosul who were partisans of Saladin, and that the final agreement was due
   to Mujahid ad-Din Qaymaz. Neither Abu Shama nor Ibn al-Athir mentions
   the cession of Bain al-Nahrain (on which see de Slane's note in R.H.C., Or.,
   II, 2, 350, and G. Le Strange, *Lands of the Eastern Caliphate*, repr. London,
   1966, 100) and Baha mentions only this (making no refrence to the cession
   of the eastern territories by 'Izz ad-Din), adding that Saladin took it from
   Sanjarshah (whose principality of Jazirat ibn 'Umar adjoined it on the
   northeast).

2. William of Tyre, XXII, cc. 1–3 (trans., II, 447–9).

was recalled by an energetic counterattack on Transjordan by Farrukhshah from Damascus. This was bad enough, but Saladin made no move until Reynald seized a caravan on its way from Damascus to Mecca. After all efforts to repair the wrong had failed, he took the field in the spring of 1182. Though his forces were not yet strong enough for a decisive blow, he no doubt hoped to inflict some further losses on the Franks. Baldwin's defensive tactics, however, prevented a major engagement but left the countryside open to the raids of Farrukhshah's cavalry, with the booty from which the Muslim forces retired well-content to Damascus.

Saladin's next operation was of a more audacious kind. As early as 1177 he had begun to reorganize the Egyptian fleet, making it a separate and independent department under its own head, with powers to take all the materials and impress all the men that it needed, and at the same time raising its grades of pay.[1] By the middle of the same year, the 'fleets of Alexandria and Damietta' were already engaged in raiding,[2] and in 1179 they carried out a daring attack on 'Akka and the Syrian coast, 'such as no Muslim fleet had ever been known to make'.[3] The seizure of Aradus in the following year has already been mentioned. In the general reorganization of the Egyptian forces

---

1. 'Imad and Ibn Ab Tayyi', *apud* Abu Shama, I, 269; most of the details are supplied by Ibn Abi Tayyi'. The raising of the rates of pay is reported by Al-Maqrizi, *Suluk*, I, 45; the *dinar al-ustul* (i.e., proportion of pay and allowance given to naval personnel in relation to the assessed value of the fiefs allotted to them) was raised from five-eighths to three-quarters. The qualities of the men presssed into the navy are severely judged by 'Imad after the defeat of the fleet before Tyre in 1187: 'Imad, *Fath*, 81.

2. 'Imad, *apud* Abu Shama, I, 270.

3. Dispatch of al-Fadl quoted Abu Shama, II, 13–14. In this dispatch (p. 14, l. 1) and in the report by Ibn Jubair (ed. G.M.S., p. 59, l. 20) special mention is made of the Maghribi sailors recruited for the fleet.

that Saladin made in 1181, the fleet was still further strengthened.[1] He now planned a combined land and sea operation against Beirut in the hope of taking it by surprise. The plan was skilfully carried out, but the garrison held off his assaults until Baldwin was ready to relieve them, when Saladin, who had come out only with light raiding, equipment, withdrew, reassembled his forces at Ba'albak, and marched northwards.[2]

During the campaigns in Mesopotamia and the struggle for Aleppo, Farrukhshah was left in Damascus with instructions to meet as best he could with the troops at his disposal the raids made by the Franks into the Muslim territories. 'While they knock down villages', said Saladin, as news of Baldwin's raids into Hawran reached him, 'we are taking cities.'[3] Much more

---

1. See n. 1 above. Summary notices of the measures for strengthening the fleet in this year are preserved by Al-Maqrizi, *Suluk.* I, 73.

2. In the absence of the narrative in *Barq* of 'Imad ad-Din, on which the brief statement in Abu Shama, II, 29, is based, the fullest account is that of William of Tyre, XXII, cc. 17–18 (trans. II, 475–9), who raises the question of Saladin's object in making the raid, for it seems improbable that he should have intended to hold Beirut, which as an isolated and not naturally strong fortress lying between Jerusalem and Tripoli would have been untenable in these circumstances. It is just conceivable that he may have had plans at this stage to use Beirut as a base for more extensive operations against either Tripoli or Jerusalem, and to widen his holding sufficiently to establish a corridor to the coast. But the troops at his disposal were obviously too few to hold an exposed position of this kind. It is certain from our documentation that Saladin was convinced that no decisive action was possible in Palestine until Aleppo was brought under his control and he could utilize also the Mesopotamian forces; and since it is probable that he had already determined to march on Aleppo in the course of this year, he could not extend his forces in the south, but on the contrary had to concentrate them. The evidence consequently seems to point to the conclusion that the attack on Beirut was conceived simply as a raid.

3. The phrase is quoted by Ibn al-Athir, XI, 219, and may be no more than *ben trovato*. But William of Tyre, XXII, 20 (trans., II, 481) makes no secret of the fact that the Franks regarded the absence of Saladin's army as =

serious was the news of Reynald's commerce-raiding in the Red Sea and penetration into the Hijaz in February 1183. Saladin's admiral, Husam ad-Din Lu'lu', taught the raiders a drastic lesson but not before the report of the exploit sent a thrill of consternation and horror round the Muslim world, and very probably did as much as any other single event to enhance Saladin's reputation and strengthen his position.[1]

The expeditions in the latter half of 1183, already mentioned, were inconclusive in one sense, but served to throw the Franks back on the defensive.[2] The equally unsuccessful siege of Karak in August 1184 and subsequent raid on Palestine served one useful purpose nevertheless, in that it brought together for the first time most of the diverse contingents of Saladin's army and gave them some much-needed practice in combined operations. The Egyptian fleet also continued its activities in both of these years, although in less spectacular ways.[3] Raymond of Tripoli and the barons were, therefore, ready enough to ask for the armistice which, in the spring of 1185, freed Saladin for his final campaign against Mosul.[4]

= an opportunity for ravaging rather than for attempting any substantial conquest, and that they were not a little indignant at the way in which he turned his back on them.

1. See, e.g., Ibn Jubair, 59, who was present during the parade of prisoners at Alexandria in the following May. The main account of the episode is that given by 'Imad, *Barq*, V, ff. 42 sqq., very adequately summarized by Abu Shama, II, 35.

2. William of Tyre, XXIII, preface (trans., II, 506): 'In punishment for our sins the enemy has become stronger than ourselves and we who used to triumph over our foes and customarily bore away the glorious palm of victory now, deprived of divine favour, retire from the field in ignominious defeat after nearly every conflict'.

3. 'Imad, *apud* Abu Shaa, II, 47; Maqrizi, *Suluk*, I, 88.

4. The main authority is Ernoul (*Chronique d'Ernoul et de Bernard le trésorier*, ed. Mas Latrie, Paris, 1871, 124), who attributes Raymond's action to the failure of the harvest and threat of famine, and adds that Saladin immediately supplied the Christians with ample stocks of food, whereby =

Saladin's most conspicuous weakness was in the field of administration. Each extension of his territories involved the selection of a governor who would maintain his own principles and loyally cooperate in the great design. But across this there cut the intense loyalty that he felt towards the members of his family, a trait in him that was perhaps reinforced by his Kurdish origin. He gave them his complete confidence and expected of them an equal confidence and loyalty in return. Himself completely indifferent to the material rewards of power, he seems to have had no conception of the corrupting influence of power and wealth on others, and it was, apparently, not until his serious illness in 1185 that he became fully aware of the jealousies amongst them. His general practice was, therefore, to confer full and uncontrolled authority on his viceroys, only

---

= Raymond acquired great popularity. The only direct mention of the armistice in the Muslim sources is in Kamal ad-Din (III, 80; Blochet, 95), but it is referrd to by 'Imad, Abu Shama, II, 75; the original has been misunderstood by Ibn al-Athir, XI, 348, and presented as a separate truce with Raymond). The bearing of the armistice has been misrepresented both by Lane-Poole and by Grousset. The former (*Saladin*, 181) asserts that 'With Raymond it was more than a truce; it was an offensive and defensive alliance. Saladin was to support him in his designs on the crown.' This anticipates the events of 1186–7, and has no authority whatsoever in the sources. Grousset's comment is still more astonishing: 'La conclusion de cette trève prouve que Saladin, satisfait de la constitution de son vaste empire syro-égyptien, en arrivait, malgré ses proclamations en faveur de la guerre sainte, a tolérer pratiquement l'établissement franque de Sahel' (Grousset, *Histoire des Croisades*, Paris, 1934–6, II, 761). It would be impossible to misunderstand Saladin's character more completely. This is to restate the cynical view that is represented by Ibn al-Athir, and even to enlarge on it, for even Ibn al-Athir never doubts Saladin's ultimate object. It may be asked further what was the 'satisfaction' that the mere constitution of a empire gave to him. In a letter written after the occupation of Aleppo he had said: 'Our desire in the possession of territories is their men, not their money, their military force, not the abundance of their goods, their readiness to engage the enemy, not their material comforts' (Abu Shama, II, 43), and there is not a single action of his career which conflicts with this declaration.

requiring them to promise just and equitable treatment of their subjects in the spirit of the *Shari'a*, a contribution to the war-chest of the *jihad*, and the maintenance of their regiments in good order and discipline, in readiness to set out when they were called for.[1] So far as the latter condition is concerned, it seems to have been duly observed, except by Turanshah, whose record both in Yemen and Damascus had been lamentable. The first condition was by no means so generally executed. The vast fortunes left by governors and officers, such as Nasir ad-Din at Hims,[2] allow us to deduce a state of affairs of which we can sometimes find precise evidence.[3] That Saladin was aware of abuses is evident from the frequent prohibitions of 'illegal' taxes and other oppressive practices in his rescripts and diplomas, and occasional specific references to the conduct of

---

1. On Turanshah's power at Damascus see p.23, n. 4 above. Similarly, 'Imad says of al-'Adil's government in Egypt: وهو مستقل بالأمر والنهي . . . وإبرام المعاقد وإحكام القواعد. . . . وهو سلطان الديار المصرية على الحقيقة . . . وهو يمده بالمال والرجال ('Imad, *Barq*, V, f. 116b.) The terms of Ibn al-Muqaddam's diploma as governor of Damascus ('Imad, *Barq*, V, 46b; 47a) present even more clearly the principles of Saladin's administration. *Michel le syrien*, III, 409, 410, says categorically that Taqi ad-Din, al-'Adil, and Saladin's three sons al-Afda (Damascus), al-'Aziz (Egypt) and az-Zahir, (Aleppo) were called by the title of sultan.

2. 'Imad, *apud* Abu Shama, II, 69. It in this connection that Ibn al-Athir (XI, 341) finds, for the one and only time, an occasion to charge Saladin with the appropriaton of property. After relating, in the authority of some unnamed persons, but with a repudiation of any personal responsibility for the story (ذكروا وعليهم العهدة), that Nasir ad-Din was poisoned at Saladin's instigation, he states as a fact that Saladin reviewed his cousin's possessions and 'took most of them, leaving for his son only what was useless', and embroiders the story with a malicious tailpiece, introduced, significantly, by 'And I have heard that ...' (وبلغني أن). But 'Imad, who was an eyewitness, states categorically that Saladin had Nasir ad-Din's possessions inventoried and divided the whole of them in the legal proportions between his widow, his son and his daughter, 'without bestowing a single glance on them'.

3. E.g. Ibn al-Muqaddam during his tenure of Ba'albak: أقام بها مستقرّا ولأخلاف أعمالها مستــدزا ('Imad *apud* Abu Shama, II, 2). Also the well-known passage of Ibn Jubair (G.M.S. 301–2), on which see C. Cahen, 'Indigènes et croisés' in *Syria*, Paris, 1934, 356 sqq.

fiefholders.[1] But he had little patience with the perpetual and petty, but necessary, details of daily administration, and the lack of his personal supervision made itself felt.[2]

From the time he left Egypt to occupy Damascus in 1175, his viceroy there had been his brother Saif ad-Din al-'Adil, and in 1179 his nephew Farrukhshah had replaced Turanshah in Damascus. Farrukhshah's brother Taqi ad-Din 'Umar held Hamah and its northern dependencies, and still had hopes of an African empire. In 1182 the state of anarchy in Yemen led to the appointment of Saladin's brother Tughtagin as viceroy in that province, and on Farrukhshah's death in the same year Ibn al-Muqaddam was reinstated as governor of Damascus.[3] The occupation of Aleppo in 1183 involved a major reorganization.[4] Saladin at first invested his own son aZ-Zahir Ghazi 'as sultan'[5] with a number of trusted officers to support him, but this arrangement was challenged by al-'Adil, who asked that he might exchange the government of Egypt for that of Aleppo. Whatever Saladin's regrets at deposing his favourite son may

---

1. In the diploma appointing Ibn al-Muqaddam as governor of Damascus in 578/1182–3 he is explicitly enjoined to restrain the fiefholders from oppressing the countrymen, 'Imad, *Barq*, V, f. 47b: كافا للمقطعين من ظلم أهل الضياع.
2. See, for example, 'Imad's statement on the revenue accounts at Damascus, Abu Shama, II, 5 (from 'Imad, *Barq*, III, 105b–106a).
3. His diploma of appointment (see p. 49, n. 3), after instructing him to 'review the troops, keep them in good condition, compel them to maintain the numbers and equipment of their fighting men, and see that no one absents himself except by permission for good and sufficient reason' and to maintain order among the Arab tribes, adds: 'And if any of the Arabs remain in the territory of the Franks, he shall dispatch the *'askar* to them and continue to harass them until they are brought into submission by desire or fear.'
4. The statement that Saladin had intended to appoint his youngest brother Taj al-Muluk Buri as governor of Aleppo has only the dubious backing of Ibn al-Athir, XI, 328. There does not seem to be any reference in 'Imad's work to the subject.
5. The phrase in that of Ibn Abi Tayyi', *apud* Abu Shama, II, 47. He was born in Egypt in 568 and was therefore only fifteen years old at this time.

have been, he agreed without demur, and the diploma of appointment, which was drawn up in terms of brotherly affection unusual for such formal documents, conferred on al-'Adil unrestricted authority, subject to the usual stipulations that he should furnish a fixed sum for the arsenal and treasury of the *jiha* and a fixed number of foot-soldiers.[1] On the advice of his trusted counsellor, the Al-Qadi al-Fadil,[2] he replaced al-'Adil in Egypt by Taqi ad-Din 'Umar, but with a well-justified fear of his impetuosity reluctantly sent the Qadi with him to exercise a moderating influence.[3]

During his grave illness, several of his relatives, anticipating his death, began to make dispositions in their own interests. Partly because of this, partly because he was anxious to establish his own sons, now in their teens,[4] he distributed the provinces in 1186. Al-'Adil, on his own suggestion, was reappointed to Egypt, not, however, in full possession but as guardian of Saladin's son al-'Aziz 'Uthman. Taqi ad-Din took his deposition in bad part, and for a moment threatened to go out west, taking with him a large part of the Egyptian army.

---

1. The *manshur* is transcribed in full in 'Imad, *Barq*, V, ff. 124a–126a. By 'foot-soldiers' are meant, in all probability, siege-troops, who are actually found accompanying the *'askar* of Aleppo to the siege of Tyre ('Imad, *Fath*, 75). Ibn Abi Tayyi' , *apud* Abu Shama, II, 52, asserts that al-'Adil wished Saladin to draw up a contract of sale for Aleppo, but he refused, saying 'Do you imagine that cities are bought and sold?.'

2. 'Imad, *Barq*, V, f. 117b.

3. 'Imad, *Barq*, V, f. 120b, followed by the text of the *manshur* (in much more formal terms), ff. 121a–122b. Taqi ad-Din retained at the same time his fief of Hamah. The exchange was carried through at the siege of Karak in 1183, when al-'Adil came up from Egypt with his contingent, and Taqi ad-Din and his personal troops went back with it.

4. Ibn Khallikand (No. 856, *Wafayat al-a'yan*, XII, 58; de Slane, IV, 511 (also R.H.C., Or., III, 411)) relates a story that one of his officers reproached him on his recovery for appointing his brothers to all the great fiefs and leaving his sons unsupported.

Nevertheless, he at length obeyed Saladin's order to present himself in Damascus and was reappointed to his fiefs in the north, together with Mayyafariqin in Diyar Bakr. Aleppo was restored to aZ-Zahir Ghazi.[1]

In any estimate of Saladin's career the chief place must be given to the efforts by which he built up the material power now about to be discharged upon the Franks with accumulated force. But there was another, less obvious, group of activities which were being prosecuted at the same time and to the same end. The extent to which Saladin's diplomacy was employed to isolate the Franks in Syria and to ensure that as far as possible he should be on terms of peace, if not of friendship, with every external potential antagonist before opening his decisive campaign, has not been sufficiently appreciated. It was directed on two fronts.

The Muslims in Syria and Egypt were well aware of the large place that the trading interests of the Italian republics represented in the maintenance of the Latin states, and of the rivalries between Pisa, Genoa and Venice. From the beginning of his government Saladin made efforts to attract their trade to Egypt, trade that, in view of his control of the Red Sea, might have the double advantage of increasing his own resources and diminishing the value of the Syrian trade. The earliest treaty which has so far been attested was one with Pisa in 1173,[2] and its utility was demonstrated in the following year, when the Pisans and other European merchants assisted the Egyptian forces against the Sicilians at Alexandria.[3] Saladin's own letter to

---

1. 'Imad, *apud* Abu Shama, II, 69–70; Baha'; 64–5. When, however, Taqi ad-Din summoned his troops from Egypt to rejoin him, he detached his mamluk Yuzaba with a cavalry force to join Qaraqush in the Maghrib.

2. Heyd, *Histoire du commerce du Levant*, I, 387.

3. Heyd, I, 398, n. 1. In the same note the dates of three other letters written =

Baghdad on this occasion affirms the existence of treaties with Genoa and Venice as well: 'There is not one of them but supplies our land with its materials of war ... and treaties of peaceful intercourse have been negotiated with them all.'[1] Three years later, a letter from al-Fadil to Saladin refers in passing to 'the envoys of the different peoples' in Cairo,[2] and there can be no doubt that this trade greatly assisted the reconstruction of the Egyptian fleet.

Still more effective for Saladin's purpose were the diplomatic negotiations with Constantinople. The efforts of the Greeks to persuade the Latins in Syria to cooperate in attacks on Egypt constituted a standing threat to its security. At the same time, it was difficult to reach an agreement with them, without turning the Seljuqs of Anatolia against him. The disaster inflicted on Manuel's army by Qilij Arslan at Myriakephalon in 1176, however, ended for a time direct hostilities between them, and on Manuel's death in 1180 his successors took the initiative in opening relations with Saladin, which were affirmed by a treaty in 1181. The growing hostility between the Greeks and Latins increased the utility and frequency of these relations, which were maintained between Saladin and both Isaac Angelus at Constantinople and Isaac Comnenus in Cyprus.[3] Such terms of

---

= to Pisa by Saladin or by al-'Adil are quoted, from 572/1176, 574/1179 and 575/1180.

1. Abu Shama, I, 243 The date of this letter was 1174, and not 1182, as stated by Heyd's source, Amari.

2. 'Imad, *Barq*, III, f. 50b, letter dated Dhu'l-Hijja 573 (May–June 1177): من بالباب من رسل الأمم المخالفة. See also J. Hartman, *Die Personlichkeit Saladin...*, Berlin, 1933, 59; and ibid., 55–7, for embassies between Saladin and Frederick Barbarossa.

3. Cf. C. Cahen, *Syrie du nord*, 422–5; Rohricht, Geschichte des Konigreichs Jerusalem, 1100–1291, Innsbruck, 1898, 493–4. The report from a Latin source of the terms agreed on between Saladin and Andronicus Comnenus (Grousset, II, 751, note) is suspect, and improbable in detail.

friendship with the traditional foes of Islam were no doubt sufficiently justified in Saladin's eyes by their immediate advantage, but they gave him the further satisfaction of restoring, if only temporarily, the old institution of Muslim worship at Constantinople in the name of the 'Abbasid caliph.[1]

By the end of 1186 everything was organized and ready for the signal. But Saladin was still bound by the terms of the treaty of 1185 and had to wait until he was furnished with a *casus belli*. A promising opening had been offered by the conflict between Raymond of Tripoli and Guy, and the ensuing alliance between Raymond and the sultan.[2] Some of his troops were actually sent to reinforce the garrison of Tiberias[3]; consequently, Guy's first intention, urged on by the master of the Templars, to attack Tiberias would have had the effect of setting the war in motion. Early in 1187 Reynald of Karak made his fatal blunder of attacking a Meccan trading caravan in violation of his engagements, and refused to yield up his booty in response either to the threats of Saladin or the appeals of the king. Saladin, vowing vengeance, issued the summons to all his viceroys and vassals, and himself set out with his guard on 14 March to protect the return of the pilgrim caravan. The Egyptian contingent, arriving after some delay, joined in ravaging the lands of Karak and Shawbak, and returned with him to

---

1. Baha', Schultens, 129–30 = Cairo, 115–16 and 'Imad, *apud* Abu Shama, II, 159 inf. It is probable that this had not been done since the beginning of the Crusades.

2. 'Imad, *Fath*, 17–18, and Abu Shama, II, 74. Ibn al-Athir, XI, 347–8, gives a reconstruction of this passage, adding the implausible statement that 'Saladin guaranteed that he would make him the future king of all the Franks'. 'Imad says only that 'Raymond whipped up the Sultan's determination to attack them, that he might restore the kingdom to him'.

3. Ernoul, 142, 152. The same situation is implied in 'Imad, *Fath*, 18, ll. 8–19. The comparison with Ernoul shows how accurately 'Imad presents the facts of the situation.

Damascus, two months later; meanwhile, the contingents from Damascus, Aleppo, Mesopotamia, Mosul and Diyar Bakr assembled at Ra's al-Ma', and raided the country of Tiberias.[1] At Saffuriya a body of Templars and Hospitallers, disregarding Raymond's instructions, engaged a powerful force making a demonstration raid on 1 May, and were killed or captured almost to a man.[2]

At the end of May Saladin reviewed the combined forces at 'Ashtara in Hawran. The regular cavalry contingents mustered twelve thousand, with possibly as many again of auxiliary troops and irregulars,[3] To each amir he assigned his place on the left or right wing, from which he might not depart; no contingent must absent itself, nor a single man leave. From each

---

1. His son al-Afdal was left at Ra's al-Ma' to marshal the incoming troops. The Aleppo contingent was commanded by Dilderim al-Yaruqi; those of the Jazira, Mosul and Diyar Bakr by Geukburi; and that of Damascus by Qaymaz an-Najmi: 'Imad, *apud* Abu Shama, II, 75–6.

2. The vivid and first-hand account of Ernoul, 144–8, seems substantially trustworthy, and is confirmed in its general lines by 'Imad, *Fath*, 14. Since the latter mentions the presence of all three of the commanders named in n. 3 at the engagement, Ernoul's figure of six or seven thousand horsemen is correct. Ernoul adds that it was only after the meeting between Balyan and Raymond after the battle (p. 152) that the Saracens were driven out of Tiberias.

3. On the basis of the figures which are to be found in scattered references in the soures, the distribution of the various contingents may be estimated with fair accuracy as follows:

Saladin's personal guard	1,000
Egyptian Contingent	4,000
'Askar of Damascus	1,000
'Askar of Aleppo	1,000
Mesopotamia, Mosul, and Diyar Bakr contingents	5,000

   There is no indication at all in the Arabic sources of the numbers of auxiliary troops, foot-soldiers and irregulars, but their presence at the Battle of Hattin is casually attested, in particular by 'Imad's statement that the grass was set on fire by 'some of the volunteers for the Holy War' (بعض مطّوعة المجاهدين).

company he picked out the advance guard of archers ... and said: "When we enter the enemy's territory, this is the order of our forces and these the positions of our companies."[1] On Friday, 26 June, he set out for Palestine and after a halt of five days at Uqhuwana, at the south end of the lake, advanced into the hills above Tiberias. While the two armies lay opposite one another, Saladin, whether by accident or design, led his guards and siege personnel to Tiberias on Thursday, 2 July. Raymond's countess held the castle against his assault, but her appeal to Guy for help secured the opportunity that had been denied to him for all these years, a set encounter in the field with the forces of the Kingdom.[2]

The overwhelming character of the victory at Hattin (4 July)[3] was proved immediately by the tale of cities and fortresses that

---

1. 'Imad, *Fath*, 19.
2. It is well known from Ernoul's narrative (158–62) that Raymond himself opposed the advance and that Guy gave the signal for it on the persuasion of the master of the Temple. 'Imad in his epic but, of course, imaginative presentation of the scene in the Crusaders' camp, pictures Raymond as the instigator of the march and precisely reverses his argument ('Imad, *Fath*, 22: ولما سمع القومص بفتح طبرية . . . قال لهم لا قعود بعد اليوم ولا بد لنا من وقم القوم فإذا أُخذت طبرية أُخذت البلاد وذهبت الطراف والتلاد. On the other hand his statement as to Saladin's reception of the news can be taken at face value: 'He was rejoiced on learning of their advance and said "At last we have go what we want" وسر حين أحاط بميسرهم علمه وقال قد حصل المطلوب It is interesting that Ibn al-Athir (XI, 352), also developing the theme on his customary lines of imaginary dialogue, hits off Raymond's attitude correctly, at least in the first part of the argument.
3. On the battle itself there is little to be added to the narratives of Rohricht (Geschichte, 431–41) or Lane-Poole (*Saladin*, 208–15). (Grousset, II, 791–9, is less objective.) *Michel le syrien*, III, 404, adds the imaginative detail that Saladin, after killing Arnald with his own hand and the 300 'phrer' (i.e., Templars), 'took a bath in their blood'. 'Imad, *Fath*, adds two details: Saladin took Reynald of Karak prisoner, but handed him to an attendant to kill him, and there is a grim account of the slaughter of a hundred of the Templars and Hospitallers ('Imad, *Fath*, 29).

fell either to Saladin personally ('Akka,[1] Tibnin, Sidon,[2] Beirut[3]) or to separate contingents under their generals (such as Nazareth, Caesarea and Nablus). Then, passing Tyre for the time being,[4] he joined forces with al-'Adil (who had already stormed Jaffa) and besieged Ascalon, which was surrendered on 5 September, on his promise to release Guy and the master of the Temple, a promise duly fulfilled. The remaining castles in this region were captured either on the march to Ascalon or just afterwards. Finally, reuniting his armies, Saladin advanced to the goal of his ambitions, the capture of Jerusalem. After a siege of less than a fortnight the city surrendered on 2 October, on terms that confirmed – if confirmation were needed – his reputation

1. 'Akka, captured on Thursday, 9 July, was given in fief to Saladin's eldest son al-Afdal, who was born in 565/1170–1 (Abu Shama, I, 276), and after the evacuation of its inhabitants their houses and treasures were given to the troops: 'Imad, *Fath*, 31. Ibn al-Athir, XI, 355–6 et seqq., is mostly a transcript of 'Imad.

2. Captured Wednesday, 21 Jumada I (29 July): 'Imad, *Fath*, 37.

3. Captured Thursday, 29 Jumada I (6 August), after a week's siege: 'Imad, *Fath*, 38. Both Sidon and Beirut were given in fief to the Kurdish amir 'Ali al-Mashtub. 'Imad, *Fath*, 73.

4. Ernoul, 179–83, has a circumstantial account of Saladin's negotiations with the inhabitants of Tyre, their readiness to surrender, and the delivery of the city by the sudden arrival of Conrad, followed by a brief and unsucessful siege by Saladin on his way to Ascalon. Conrad's arrival at 'Akka after its capture and his stratagem to ensure his escape seems to have been a well-known story and is related in much the same terms by 'Imad (*Fath*, 43). But this historian is positive that Saladin made no attempt to attack Tyre on this occasion: *Fath*, 44: وهو البيت المقدس . . . مالهى عن طلبها طلبُ ما هو أشرف; and also below: وجاء إلى صور ناظراً إليها وعابراً عليها غير مكترث بأمرها. Baha' also (Schultens, 72 = Cairo, 65) relates that Saladin avoided a siege of Tyre 'because the army was dispersed throughout Palestine, each man taking something for himself'. Neither Baha' nor 'Imad were with Saladin at the time, however, the latter having retired to Damascus to recuperate from an illness. Ernoul's statement is certainly false in the last particular, that on leaving Tyre Saladin captured Caesarea, since this town had already been captured by the Aleppo troops under Dilderim al-Yaruqi and Ghars ad-Din Qilij ('Imad, *Fath*, 33).

for limitless courtesy and generosity.[1] The collapse of the Kingdom encouraged Saladin to hope that Tyre too might be captured before the winter began, and he laid siege to the city on 13 November. But the tenacious defence of Conrad disheartened the eastern contingents, who, now that winter was at hand, were eager to return home with their booty. A disastrous defeat of the Egyptian blockading fleet at the end of December strengthened their opposition, and in spite of Saladin's arguments for perseverance, supported by the commanders of the Aleppo regiments,[2] the amirs took their men off and dispersed, Taqi ad-Din and the armies of Mosul, Sinjar and Diyar Bakr in the lead, 'every bird of them longing for his nest, and not knowing that this short repose would be followed for them by bitter toil'.[3] On 1 January Saladin found himself

---

1. The main source in again Ernoul, 211–35, the details of whose description are sufficiently familiar from the standard works. 'Imad (*Fath*, 56) gives the total sum received by the treasury in ransoms as about 100,000 dinars, but does not spare the rascality of its Egyptian and Syrian agents.

2. 'Imad, *Fath*, 88.

3. Ibid., 90. There can be no doubt on any historical principles that this account is the true one. It was written by one in intimate touch with the events; it is fortified by named and precise details, and its statements are wholly consistent with the persons concerned. It is difficult to understand why, with this original text before their eyes, so many historians (Rohricht, Geschichte, 470, is an exception) have disregarded it in favour of Ibn al-Athir's derivative and partisan account (XI, 468) which, by deliberate inversion of the paragraphs relating Saladin's discontinuance of the siege and the withdrawal of the amirs, places the events in a false light and attempts to excuse the action of the Mosul commanders by throwing the blame on Saladin's shoulders. This is by no means a unique example of Ibn al-Athir's 'editorial' methods, as has been seen in the notes above. An even more blatant example of the same kind is found in his account of the relief of the garrison of 'Akka during the winter of 1190 (XXI, 35–6). This entire passage is taken from 'Imad (*Fath*, 312–14) who indeed criticizes Saladin's decision as mistaken, though based on compassionate motives. But when 'Imad goes on to describe Saladin's energy in pressing on with the relief and urging his officers and agents to greater efforts, Ibn al-Athir sees fit to substitute an accusation of negligence on his part and dependence upon the efforts of =

compelled to relinquish the siege and retired to winter at 'Akka, where a succession of embassies brought him the congratulations of all the Muslim princes, including his former rivals in Azerbaijan and Northern Persia.[1]

Leaving 'Akka to be refortified under the charge of his trusted mamluk Baha' ad-Din Qaraqush, Saladin returned to Damascus in the spring, halting for a short time before the still unsubdued fortress of Kawkab (Belvoir). On 10 May he marched north with his guard to join the Mesopotamian contingents under Geukburi and 'Imad ad-Din of Sinjar, while al-'Adil remained with the Egyptian regiments to guard the south and to deal with Karak and Shawbak.[2] The Aleppo and Hamah regiments were ordered to stand on guard at Tizin against any movement on Bohemond's part.[3] The remaining forces at his disposal were

---

= his lieutenants. (Michaud, *Bibliothèque des croisades*, Paris, 1829, etc., IV, 298, in quoting this passage from Ibn al-Athir, improves it further by adding another adjective: 'L'indolence accoutumée du Sultan)'.

1. 'Imad, *Fath*, 94, 119–20. At this year's Pilgrimage, Ibn al-Muqaddam, leading a large contingent of pilgrims from Syria, appears to have asserted certain claims, as the representative of Saladin, over the leader of the 'Iraqi pilgrims during the ceremonies at 'Arafa in February 1188. A brawl between the two parties caused a number of deaths, including that of Ibn al-Muqaddam himself, to whom, however, both 'Imad (*Fath*, 101, and a more detailed narrative in *Barq*, quoted by Abu Shama, II, 123) and Ibn al-Athir (XI, 370–1) give the epithet of martyr. Ibn al-Athir's account is even more vigorous in condemnation of the 'Iraqis and their amir Tashtakin than 'Imad's. Although the latter adds that he was subsequently dismissed, the action of Ibn al-Muqaddam is one of the items in the list of complaints which, at this of all moments, the *Diwan* thought fit to adress to Saladin (Abu Shama, II, 122) including an angry protest against his 'unheard-of crime' of 'sharing' the title of *an-Nasir* with the caliph.

2. 'Imad, *Fath*, 161. He gives no date for the surrender of Karak, but it had fallen before al-'Adil's return to Damascus, since it was given to him by Saladin in exchange for Ascalon (Baha' ad-Din, Schultens, 89 = Cairo, 79). Shawbak surrendered only in the spring of 1189 (Abu Shama, II, 139).

3. Baha', Schultens, 78 = Cairo, 69–70. It was at this point that Baha' =

too light to undertake prolonged siege operations, but adequate for the capture of the isolated towns and castles of the principality, as far as its northern frontiers at Baghras and Darbsak. Although Antioch itself was not in any real danger, Bohemond in September asked for and was unwillingly granted an armistice of eight months, after which the Mesopotamian contingents returned to their homes, and Saladin to Damascus. There he was rejoined by al-'Adil with his troops, and at once besieged and captured the two remaining castles in Palestine, Safad and Kawkab.[1] After the surrender of the latter on 5 January, the rest of his forces dispersed and Saladin made a tour of inspection of his coastal fortresses from Ascalon to 'Akka.[2]

The spectacular success of Saladin in reducing the holdings of the Crusaders in Syria to three cities, Tyre, Tripoli and Antioch, with one or two outlying but doomed fortresses, within the short space of eighteen months, has led both Muslim and Western historians to regard him primarily as a great and successful general, whose victories were due to the same military qualities as those of other successful commanders of armies. This is a complete misapprehension. Saladin possessed, indeed, personal military virtues of a high order; but his victories were due to his possession of moral qualities that have little in common with those of a great general. He was a man inspired by an intense and unwavering ideal, the achievement of which involved him necessarily in a long series of military activities. Down to 1186 these activities were directed to imposing his will upon the

---

= ad-Din entered the service of Saladin and, therefore, becomes a firsthand witness for the events that he relates. For the general and special features of the northern campaign of 1188, see C. Cahen, *La Syrie du nord*, 428–30.

1. 'Imad, *Fath*, 167, relates that none of the amirs was willing to accept the castle of Kawkab, and that it was finally placed under the reluctant keeping of Qaymaz an-Najmi, the commander of the Damascus regiment.

2. 'Imad, *Fath*, 168.

prevalent feudal military system and shaping it into the instrument that his purpose required; and the preceding pages have shown that their military aspect was subordinate, in his own mind and to a large extent in practice, to the task of uniting the political forces of western Asia 'in one purpose', and imbuing them with something of his own tenacity and singleness of outlook. It was by this means, and not by superior strategic ability, that he succeeded in assembling the army that was to destroy the kingdom of Jerusalem. Even the striking campaigns of 1187 and 1188 cannot be held to prove that Saladin possessed outstanding generalship. The victory at Hattin owed more to the mistakes of the Franks than to his strategy, even when every credit is given to the skill with which the opportunity was seized. The subsequent crumbling of the inner defences of Jerusalem and Antioch demonstrate rather the fundamental weakness of the Crusading states than the military genius of the conquerors, a point emphasized by the fact that many of them fell to small detached forces.

Furthermore, these very successes were due largely to the exercise of the qualities that most sharply distinguished him from his military contemporaries. Nothing is more remarkable in the sources than his reiterated appeal from the criticisms of his officers to the principles of honour, of good faith, and of a firm religious conviction. When the turn of the Christian cities and castles came, it was chiefly because of his reputation for scrupulous observance of his plighted word and for uncalculating generosity that they surrendered so easily. Those critics who have found fault with him for allowing such numbers of knights and merchants to find a refuge in Tyre and so to build up a bridgehead there for the counterattack have usually failed to consider what the course of the Third Crusade would have been if on its arrival it had found Saladin still engaged in the task of reducing one by one the castles of the interior, without complete freedom of movement and complete security in his rear.[1] That he did not in fact capture Tyre as well was the result, partly of the accident of Conrad's arrival, and partly of the impatience and insubordination of the eastern regiments.[2]

The second of these causes illustrates sharply the persisting defects in the forces with which he had to meet the later struggle with the Crusaders. But this was still in the future, and it is unhistorical to imagine Saladin as preparing plans and disposing his forces to meet the forthcoming invasion from the west. His thought had from the beginning been concentrated upon offensive, not defensive, warfare; it was for this purpose that he had built up his armies, and it had now been largely, and brilliantly, fulfilled. Though he grieved in 1187 over the lack of staying power of his vassals before Tyre, and again in 1188 before Antioch, he saw in these no more than temporary checks, and confidently expected to make up for them in later campaigns. The first hint of the coming invasion reached him from a Sicilian sea-captain at Ladhiqiya in the autumn of 1188,[3] and so little disturbed was he by the report that he granted Bohemond a truce only until May 1189, and busied himself during the winter with preparations to attack Antioch and Tripoli,[4]

---

1. Cf the judicious observations of Stevenson, *The Crusaders in the East*, Cambridge, 1926, 255–6.

2. See p. 54, n. 4 above.

3. 'Imad, *Fath*, 143 (Abu shama, II, 128–9).

4. This is clear from the letter addressed to his brother Saif al-Islam Tughtagin in Arabia (Abu Shama, II, 136–7) in which, while he speaks of the possibility of a descent upon Egypt and Syria and the consequent necessity of keeping the Egyptian forces inside Egypt, he calls on Saif al-Islam to occupy Palestine and protect the recent conquests there, while he (Saladin) himself will engage in the siege of Antioch and Taqi ad-Din will deal with Tripoli. The various hints and references to the future campaigns against the =

In all probability, therefore, he was taken by surprise when the first convoys arrived and Guy's troops succeeded in marching to 'Akka and investing the city. From that moment his role was transformed, and he was faced with a new and grimmer task which no Muslim commander, for centuries before him, had ever attempted: the task of holding an army in the field for three years, and that with every circumstance of discouragement. Had he been no more than a leader of armies, he could not have achieved it; his feudal troops would have melted away and left the field to the Franks. But it was in this wholly unexpected conjunction that the true greatness of Saladin and the inner strength of the instrument which he had created were put to the test. He had a double conflict to wage: the external struggle with the Crusaders, and the internal struggle with the fissiparous tendencies and the instability of the feudal armies. Military genius had but a small part in the combination of qualities by which he fought the Crusade to a standstill. The long campaign was an almost unbroken succession of military reverses and disasters; his generals were openly critical, his troops often mutinous. It was by the sheer force of personality, by the undying flame of faith within him, and by his example of steadfast endurance, that he inspired the dogged resistance that finally wore down the invaders.

At the moment when the operations of the Third Crusade opened with the march of Guy to 'Akka, Saladin was at Belfort (Shaqif Arnun) to receive its expected surrender from Reynald of Sidon. The north Syrian troops had been sent to mask Antioch, and besides his own Kurdish and mamluk guards and

---

= Crusaders which are to be found in the Arabic sources (and in Ibn al-Athir in particular) were, of course, written after the event.

the troops of Damascus he had with him only the contingent of the Artuqid prince of 'Amid and a number of foot-soldiers and volunteers for the Holy War. In July he had made a reconnaissance in force towards Tyre (where some of his auxiliairies had suffered heavy losses in an unauthorized attack on the causeway) and had strengthened the defences of 'Akka. Yet it was not until he actually received news of Guy's march that he called up the contingents of his nearer vassals and, leaving a small force to blockade Belfort, moved down to 'Akka. His own plan was to cut across country and intercept the Crusaders on their march, but his officers insisted on making the long and easier detour by Tiberias and he was forced to yield to their 'inclination to do the easiest thing'.[1]

Before the siege of the town was fully formed, Saladin was able to reinforce the garrison, but by doing so he left his own forces too weak to attack the besiegers until the contingents from the east, followed by Taqi ad-Din and Geukburi, enabled him to draw up a line of battle based on Tall Kaisan.[2] During the first major engagement on 16 September, the troops on the right, commanded by Taqi ad-Din, succeeded in forcing their way into 'Akka. But their success was followed by a debate which was to

---

1. Ibn al-Athir, XII, 21, summarizing 'Imad, *Fath*, 188; and cf Baha', Schultens, 114 = Cairo, 101 (R.H.C., Or., III, 152).

2. 'Imad, *Fath*, 188–9; Baha', Schultens, 99 = Cairo, 87–8 (no mention of the arrival of the eastern contingents), 104 = Cairo, 92–3: on the right al-Afdal (with the Damascus contingent?), followed by the contingents of Aleppo, Mosul, Diyar Bakr and Nablus, with Taqi ad-Din on the extreme flank; on the left the sultan's Kurdish guard with other bodies of Kurds, followed by the contingents of Sinjar, Saladin's Turkish mamluks, with the Asadi mamluks on the flank. The centre was commanded by Saladin himself and the Kurdish *faqih* 'Isa al-Hakkari. The Egyptian army was left on guard in Egypt, in case the Crusaders should attempt another descent on it. Saladin's total of regular forces was thus probably some ten thousand in addition to unspecified numbers of foot-soldiers, volunteers and camp followers.

be renewed time and again with wearisome iteration during the campaign. Should they endeavour boldly to exploit their advantage and press home the attack against the 'unbroken wall' of the Frankish infantry? In spite of Saladin's earnest pleas, all the instincts and traditions of the regular troops were opposed to such tactics. They were cavalrymen, at home only in the open field where they had ample room for manœuvre; faced with the slow undermining of an enemy's morale and material defences by siege processes, or the keeping up of a steady pressure against an entrenched army, they were quickly discouraged, and discouragement easily passed into discontent. Men and horses must be fed and watered, battles broken off at dusk, and the main force moved back to a safe distance, where the weight of armour could be discarded under the protection of an advance guard. There were some, particularly among Saladin's own regiment of guards, in whom zeal for the Holy War overcame these tendencies to relax, but the majority, especially in the eastern contingents, felt no such compulsions and found no lack of plausible excuses for delay. Let wind, weather, famine and wounds take their toll of the enemy; meanwhile, let Saladin do everything in his power to strengthen his armies and his fleets, then finally the assailants must be crushed.[1]

Such complete confidence was felt in the outcome of the campaign, however, that the Al-Qadi al-Fadil wrote to Saladin from Egypt that the announcements of the victory had already been drafted.[2] After the defeat of the Crusaders' attack on 22 September, Saladin moved his forces up to Tall al-'Iyadiya, facing the centre of their position on Tall al-Musallaha. The

---

1. This debate and the motives of the parties are presented in detail by 'Imad, *Fath*, 190–3; more briefly by Baha', 100–1.

2. Abu Shama, II, 144.

'great battle' that followed on 4 October ended in the utter rout of the Crusaders, and for once the commanders of the Muslim armies were in agreement to exploit the victory. But the troops, in the words of 'Imad ad-Din, 'were nowhere to be seen'. When the Kurdish cavalry in the centre had been driven in panic flight by the first charge, the retainers, imagining the army to be in full retreat, had started to load up the baggage trains, and the mass of camp followers had rushed into the camp and plundered everything that could be carried away. The returning troops, finding all their possessions gone, had started off in pursuit, and it took several days to collect them together again and to restore the stolen goods to their owners.[1] But the opportunity was lost, and when the debate was resumed a week later, the counsels of delays prevailed and Saladin, himself in the grip of a malignant fever, moved back to winter quarters at al-Kharruba on 16 October, while the Crusaders dug themselves in.[2]

The contingents of Saladin's eastern and Syrian vassals were now dismissed to their homes with instructions to return in the spring. His own Kurdish guards and mamluks remained in position, together with Taqi ad-Din and his regiment; the retiring forces were replaced by a contingent of the Egyptian army under al-'Adil, and foot-soldiers from Damascus and other Syrian cities were called up to attack the Frankish infantry.[3]

Even yet, however, Saladin continued to nourish hopes that the appeal of the Holy War would bring him support of other Muslim princes. A stream of letters and dispatches went out from his camp to all quarters, contrasting the zeal of the Polytheists with the strange apathy of the Believers, and his

---

1. 'Imad, *Fath*, 206–8; Baha', Schultens, 107–8 = Cairo, 96.
2. 'Imad, *Fath*, 209–13; Lane-Poole, *Saladin*, 265–6, summarizes from Baha', Schultens, 109 = Cairo, 97.
3. 'Imad, *Fath*, 214, 219, 221.

hopes were encouraged not only (for their own purposes) by the commanders of eastern contingents, but even (and still more fallaciously) by the caliph, who promised support in return for the cession to him of Shahrizur.[1] Most of all he desired the support of the Almohad fleet, to block, if possible, the passage of the new Crusaders to Syria; but the sultan of Morocco, Abu Yusuf Ya'qub, had a long-standing grievance against Taqi ad-Din and returned no answer to this or to succeeding appeals.[2]

During the winter months Saladin's anxieties were increased by the reports received from Constantinople and Konia of the advance of the German Crusade. When in October he heard news of their arrival at Constantinople, he had dispatched the Qadi Baha' ad-Din to his eastern vassals at Sinja, Mosul and Irbil, to bid them hold their forces in readiness, and to Baghdad to appeal for reinforcements.[3] In the meantime, an Egyptian fleet reprovisioned 'Akka and strengthened the garrison with ten thousand troops and seamen to man the defences.[4] But so little did the defence of Syria interest the princes outside Saladin's dominions that the Seljuq sultan Tughril, driven out of his province of Khurasan by a revolt, chose this moment to appeal to Saladin for military aid to reinstate him.[5]

1. 'Imad, *Fath*, 205, 210, 218. As 'Imad notes (219) the most powerful of the neighbouring princes, the Shah-Arman Begtimur, so far from showing any readiness to aid Saladin, was adopting a threatening attitude towards him – possibly because of his adumbrated alliance with the caliph. As for the caliph, his whole energies were being given at the time to the capture of Takrit and other townships in Uppoer Iraq (Ibn al-Athir, XII, 2, 38), and it appears from a dispatch of Al-Qadi al-Fadil that he had actually asked Saladin for his assistance in capturing them (Abu Shaa, II, 178), as 'Imad ad-Din notes that he is opposed to Saladin's proposal to cede Shahrizur.
2. Abu Shama, 171–3, Qalqashandi, VI, 526; see Gaudefroy-Demombynes in *Mélanges René Basset*, Vol. II, Paris, 1925, 279 sqq.
3. Baha', Schultens, 110 = Cairo, 97–8.
4. 'Imad, *Fath*, 224, 227.
5. 'Imad, *Fath*, 234–5. Saladin sent an envoy to Hamadan to mediate =

The return of the Crusading fleet in the early spring of 1190 cut 'Akka off again. The Syrian contingents began to rejoin Saladin in April, together with Arab and Turkmen light horse, and the Muslim forces moved up to Tall Kaisan on the 25th.[1] During May and June the eastern contingents from Harran, Sinjar, Jazirat ibn 'Umar and Mosul arrived, followed by those of Irbil in July, and a new fleet from Egypt had entered 'Akka with fresh provisions after a naval battle on 14 June.[2] In June, however, news came of the arrival of the German Crusaders at the frontiers of Cilicia. Saladin, it would appear, had placed his hopes on a successful resistance to them by the Seljuq sultan Qilij Arslan, and the now - imminent threat from the north compelled him to deplete his forces before 'Akka by detaching all the Syrian contingents and the Turkmens on 13 July to oppose their expected advance.[3] That he had small hope of their being able to withstand the vast armies of Frederick is shown by the preparations that he began to make at the same time for a desperate defence in Palestine by destroying the defences of Tiberias, Jaffa, Arsuf, Caesarea, Sidon and Jubail.[4] Meanwhile operations at 'Akka were temporarily slowed down by the outbreak of an epidemic which seems to have been most severe among the Crusaders.[5]

= between the rivals, at the same time reiterating his request for support to Qizil Arslan of Hamadan.

1. 'Imad, *Fath*, 240.

2. 'Imad, *Fath*, 244–5, 253–4, 256.

3. 'Imad, *Fath*, 264; Baha', Schultens, 123 = Cairo, 109–10. There is just a hint in 'Imad's narrative that Saladin at first intended to march north with the whole army, but when the decision to remain at 'Akka was taken, the local Syrian princes insisted on moving to the protection of their own territories and their terrified populations.

4. 'Imad, *Fath*, 264. He was rebuked for this measure by al-Qadi al-Fadil in a dispatch quoted by Abu Shama, II, 176.

5. 'Imad, *Fath*, 265.

Fear of pestilence from the thousands of bodies killed in the infantry attack on 25 July,[1] followed by the arrival of Henry of Champagne two days later, forced Saladin to with draw the main forces to al-Kharruba (1 August), leaving only an advance-guard in the forward position of Tall al-'Iyadiya.[2] To add to his troubles he was now in desperate straits for money. The cost of so long a campaign and the unceasing outlay in weapons, food, forage, equipment, and the pay of the auxiliary troops was a contingency for which the treasuries of his feudal states were wholly unprepared and inadequate. One of the chief reasons why Saladin was so determined to hold 'Akka was that he had made it his principal arsenal and had transferred to it almost the whole military stores of Egypt and Syria.[3] Such reserves as he had acquired from time to time in the past had been spent in the campaigns to extend his control over Mesopotamia and Mosul, and in the campaigns of 1187 and 1188. Egypt was his financial mainstay; but his representative, the chancellor al-Qadi al-Fadil, had repeatedly to advise him that its resources could not be stretched indefinitely, especially as the economic life of the country was suffering severely from the interruption of trade with the European states and the drain of gold.[4] Nor was it Saladin only who was beset by these difficulties. The incessant demands of his Syrian fiefholders were beginning to cause

---

1. 'Imad, *Fath*, 272–3, estimates their losses at 9,000–10,000; Baha', Schultens, 125–8 = Cairo, III–14, indicates much the same figure with circumstantial evidence.

2. 'Imad, *Fath*, 279–80.

3. Baha', Schultens, 174 = Cairo, 156 (oddly misinterpreted in Michaud, *Bibliothèque*, IV, 313, as 'l'élite des guerriers').

4. Letters from al-Qadi al-Fadil quoted by Abu Shama, II, 166, 174–8. Hence Saladin's gratitude for such gifts as the *naft*, spear-shafts, and arrows sent to him from Baghdad, although he refused to accept the 20,000 dinars offered to him at the same time as a loan ('Imad, *Fath*, 242–3; cf. Abu Shama, II, 152).

severe distress and even disorders among the population of their provinces.[1] His mamluks and the other troops retained in the field were running up debts for the supplies of provisions and provender to an extent that was taking the edge off their enthusiasm, and despite Saladin's efforts to ease their difficulties at his own expense[2] the point was to become more and more ominously stressed in their arguments with him.[3]

The success with which the garrison of 'Akka beat off the repeated assaults of the Crusaders, and the flow of deserters from the hunger and disease that stalked the Frankish camp,[4] maintained the spirits of the army for a time. But the reports brought by the deserters of the expected arrival of the kings of France and England and of plans for a general attack induced Saladin to draw back to Shafra'amm (21 October) in spite of the return of the Syrian forces a few days earlier.[5] There are some statements attributed by Baha' ad-Din to Saladin at this time that mention the arrival of envoys from the Crusaders to discuss terms of peace, but no further indications are given in any of the sources.[6] His ill health, and the insistence of his eastern contingents on withdrawing to their homes in November,

---

1. Oppression by the fiefholders in Damascus province: al-Qadi al-Fadil, *apud* Abu Shama, II, 203; and in Nablus: ibid., 207 ('Imad, *Fath*, 443).

2. Al-Qadi al-Fadil, *apud* Abu Shama, II, 177 mid, 178 mid.; cf ibid., 162 (from 'Imad ad-Din (*Barq*): *wa'innama yuqimuna bibadhli nafaqah*) and 207. The Kurdish amir Abu'l-Haija' spent in 1190 50,000 dinars of his own.

3. Baha', Schultens, 200, 221, etc.; cf 'Imad's letter to the *diwan*: 'Imad, *Fath*, 392–3.

4. 'Imad, *Fath*, 296, 299–300.

5. 'Imad, *Fath*, 294, 296. 'Imad gives as the reason for withdrawal that the amirs, in view of the expected attack, wished to have room to engage the Crusaders at a disadvantage. Baha', Schultens, 144 = Cairo, 128–9, explains it as due to the bilious fever from which Saladin was again suffering, and which prevented him from taking part in the general engagement at Ra's al-'Ain on 13 and 14 November ('Imad, *Fath*, 302–3).

6. Baha', Schultens, 145, 147 = Cairo, 129, 131.

appear to have induced a mood of despondency in him, which is reflected in a series of letters of consolation and encouragement from al-Qadi al-Fadil,[1] who finally came to join him in person before 'Akka in January.[2]

In the same month, profiting by the withdrawal of the Crusaders' fleets, he arranged for the relief of the hard-pressed garrison of 'Akka. The operation should have been organized well in advance; improvised as it was at the last mement, it was hampered by delays and hindrances of many kinds. The civil population of the town streamed out as well as the garrison and their loss could not be made good. The regular troops were understandably reluctant to undertake an uncongenial and dangerous task; an appeal for volunteers amongst the auxiliary troops had little success; gales caused losses of ships, men and provisions; and there were financial difficulties. 'Imad ad-Din accuses civil officials in the administration of sabotage; most of them, he says, being Copts, were secret supporters of the Franks. It is more probable that, as in all bureaucracies, the obstacle was constituted by red tape rather than by ill will, in spite of Saladin's repeated and urgent appeals to set aside normal accountancy precautions at this crisis. Before the relief was completed the Crusading fleet returned, and the total garrison, now commanded by the valiant Kurdish officer al-Mashtub, was probably reduced to about a third of its former effectiveness.[3]

In spite of the criticisms that have been directed after the event to this relief of the garrison, the new defenders succeeded

---

1. Extracts in Abu Shama, II, 166–9.
2. 'Imad, *Fath*, 318.
3. The fullest narrative is in 'Imad, *Fath*, 312–14, supplemented in Abu Shaa, II, 181, from 'Imad, *Barq*: cf also Baha', Schultens, 154–5 = Cairo, 138–40, and the dispatch quoted in 'Imad, *Fath*, 366.

in holding 'Akka until July, in face of the entire Crusading army. No power that Saladin disposed of could have sufficed, in all human calculations, to save the fall of the city at this stage of events. But for Saladin himself the most cruel deception was that at this decisive moment he was both materially and morally weakened from an unexpected quarter.

In October 1190 his vassal at Irbil, Zain ad-Din, had died, and the successful competitor for his succession was his brother Geukburi,[1] who surrendered in return his Mesopotamian fiefs of Harran, Edessa and Sumaisat. These were bestowed by Saladin on his nephew Taqi ad-Din, in addition to his north Syrian fiefs. Early in March Taqi ad-Din was permitted to leave the camp with his mamluk regiment of seven hundred guards to organize his new fiefs, but with strict orders not to displace any other vassal of Saladin or to engage in any fighting, and to return with the enlarged force that he would now be able to maintain.[2] No sooner had Taqi ad-Din reached the Jazira than he attacked and expelled the allied Bogusag chiefs of Sevaverak, seized Hani, and appropriated the fiefs of Saladin's Artuqid vassal, Ibn Qara-Arslan. He then engaged and defeated the Shah-Arman Begtimur and besieged Khilat (on Lake Van) but failing to capture it, ravaged Armenia for several months and laid siege to Milazgird, where he died on 10 October 1191.[3]

The anger and dismay that Saladin felt at this reckless and insubordinate conduct of his kinsman was intensified by its

1. 'Imad, *Fath*, 298–9 and 'Imad, *Barq, apud* Abu Shama, II, 164. Geukburi undertook to pay 50,000 dinars (annually?) for his fief.
2. 'Imad, *Fath*, 322–3, 358; Baha' Schultens, 154 = Cairo, 138. Shortly before, az-Zahir returned to Aleppo with the intention of besieging Safitha. The seven hundred horsemen are explicitly mentioned by Ibn al-Athir, XII, 40–1.
3. 'Imad, *Fath*, 401–6; *Michel le syrien*, III, 408–9, who notes that he had the title of *Sultan*, and compares him as a persecutor of the Christians to Julian the Apostate; Ibn al-Athir, XII, 40–1.

immediate consequences. All his vassals in Diyar Bakr, fearing
for their lands, stayed at home instead of rejoining him before
'Akka, and even Geukburi at Irbil remained absent, engaged in
his own designs. In due course there came also a letter of
vigorous disapproval from the Caliphate, to which Saladin could
only plead in reply his repudiation of Taqi ad-Din's conduct.[1]
More than any other person, he exclaimed later, Taqi ad-Din
was reponsible for the fall of 'Akka.[2] But the consequences did
not end there; they continued to hamper him until the finish of
the struggle with Richard, since the settlement of the situation
left by Taqi ad-Din involved the absence of both aZ-Zahir and
al-'Adil during the critical campaign on the Jersualem road.

Saladin's forces during the campaign of 1191 were thus reduced
to his personal troops, the Syrian contingents, the troops of Sinjar,
and Partial contingents from Egypt and Mosul, most of which
arrived only in the latter part of June.[3] On 4 June he had moved up
to Tall al-'Iyadiya, and in spite of the consternation caused by the
arrival of Richard immediately afterwards,[4] kept up a regular
offensive against the Crusaders' lines. After the failure of the
general assault on 3 July, when the Muslim cavalry were unable to
confront the 'wall of arms' formed by the Crusading infantry,[5] he

---

1. 'Imad, *Barq*, quoted in Abu Shama, II, 183; Baha' Schultens, 213 = Cairo, 191–3.

2. 'Imad, *Fath*, 358.

3. 'Imad, *Fath*, 326, 343–4. A portion of the army of Mosul was engaged, on Saladin's orders, in besieging Jazirat ibn 'Umar from April to August, in order to punish its Zangrid prince Sanjarshah, who had left the camp before 'Akka in the previous year without permission (Ibn al-Athir, XII, 38–40; cf 'Imad, *Fath*, 298–9, and 'Imad, *Barq, apud* Abu Shama, II, 165). The forces of Shaizar and Hims, and the Turkmens under Dilderim whom Saladin had hired, arrived between 8 and 10 July ('Imad, *Fath*, 557), as 'Akka was on the point of surrender.

4. 'Imad, *Fath*, 336.

5. 'Imad, *Fath*, 350–1; Baha' Schultens, 174 = Cairo, 156–7.

realized that the end was at hand, and instructed the garrison to break out on the night of the 4th. The whole army stood under arms all night to support the evacuation, but the plan miscarried through delays within the town and the leakage of the project through deserters.[1] Nothing now remained but to arrange terms for its surrender, when the garrison capitulated on its own terms on 12 July.

Although the capture of 'Akka was a resounding victory for the Crusaders (which was to be thrown into still stronger relief by the part it played in the following century) yet the balance-sheet of the long struggle was not unfavourable to Saladin. In the absence of adequate statistical data on the numbers and casualties on both sides, it is difficult to reach precise conclusions on the military losses involved. The Muslims might console themselves by placing the losses of the Franks at not less than fifty thousand,[2] but even if the casualties in battle were less unequal, it is clear that the losses among the Crusading forces from pestilence and famine were far greater than among the Muslims, and may have outnumbered their losses in battle. Much more important is the consideration that Saladin's tenacity, by pinning the Crusaders down to this single enterprise for nearly two years, fatally weakened their first offensive power, gave time for psychological fissures to widen and to disrupt their unity, and thus finally saved the situation. Furthermore, the losses on the Muslim side were more easily recuperated; and the fact that the stream of fresh contingents from Europe had dried up before the war of movement was renewed was not without its effects on the morale of both sides.

On the other hand, the defeat before 'Akka did much to

---

1. 'Imad, *Barq, apud* Abu Shama, II, 187; 'Imad, *Fath*, 355.

2. 'Imad, *Fath*, 360.

weaken Saladin's control over the regular troops, and so to weaken their fighting power as an army. Their loss of confidence in his generalship (or in his luck) and their open disgust with the long, heavy and unrewarding campaign, with nothing to show for it but mounting debts and the exhaustion of men and animals, placed him at a serious disadvantage. They refused to garrison any fortress, in case (they argued) they would be left to suffer the fate of the garrison of 'Akka. They were seldom willing to engage in general combat in the open field. Thus the only tactics open to him were essentially the same as those to which he had been reduced at 'Akka: to contain the Crusading force to the best of his ability and hope to wear them down by the tenacity of his defence.

While the parleys and negotiations were dragging out to their tragic end on 20 August with Richard's slaughter of the Muslim prisoners,[1] Saladin was actively calling up fresh troops, and after the massacre renewed his appeals to the deaf ears of the Muslim princes.[2] Urgent summonses were sent out to his Artuqid vassals and to Geukburi at Irbil,[3] and his envoy at the Almohad court was instructed to inform the sultan that the struggle would continue and that his naval support was more necessary than ever.[4] When the march down the coast began, the Al-Qadi al-Fadil was sent to Damascus to give instructions to the expected reinforcements[5]; but Taqi ad-Din was still operating in Upper Mesopotamia, and there is no record of their arrival.

1. Both 'Imad (*Fath*, 373) and Baha' (Schultens, 183 = Cairo, 164–5) give this date. In regard to the negotiations there is little to add to Stevenson's discussions (*The Crusaders in the East*, 269–73). It is noteworthy that when Louis left for Tyre, Saladin, learning of his departure, 'sent an envoy after him with gifts suitable to his rank': 'Imad, *Fath*, 371.
2. Dispatch from 'Imad, *Barq*, quoted *apud* Abu Shama, II, 190.
3. 'Imad, *Fath*, 364–8.
4. Abu Shama, II, 188–9.
5. 'Imad, *Barq, apud* Abu Shama, II, 190.

As soon as the direction of Richard's march was known, Saladin sent out scouts to select suitable places on the coast road where the Crusaders might be attacked on the march.[1] The ill humour of his troops at the outset was displayed in their unwillingness to support al-Afdal in his attack on the Crusaders' rearguard during the march from 'Akka to Haifa;[2] but in harrying the Crusaders on the march, they were more in their element. The unfamiliar type of defence put up by an organized and disciplined infantry defeated their normal tactics, and the attempt to smash through it by sheer mass in the organized general attack at Arsuf (7 September) only threw them off their balance before the sudden counterattack of the cavalry. The famous battle is described in epic style and with legendary detail in the *Itinerary*,[3] and with some exaggeration even by Baha' ad-Din, since he himself subsequently records that the contingents of Aleppo, Damascus and Mosul stood firm when Saladin's own squadrons fled before the charge of the knights.[4] The decisive stroke on which Saladin had counted was beaten off and turned into a near defeat; but the Muslim forces remained intact after

---

1. 'Imad, *Fath*, 374.
2. 'Imad, *Fath*, 376; Baha'; Schultens, 185 = Cairo, 166, gives a different version.
3. *Itinerarium Peregrinorum et* Gesta Regis Ricardi (ed. Stubbs), Rolls Series, London, 1864, IV, cc. 18–22. The legendary element is especially obvious in relating the attack of Taqi ad-Din, who was engaged with Begtimur in Armenia at the time, and in the speeches of Saladin and 'Sanscunsus' of Aleppo.
4. Baha', Schultens, 196–7 = Cairo, 175–7; cf. 'Imad, *Fath*, 385. There is a curious phrase in 'Imad's letter to the *diwan* which looks like an oblique rebuke to Saladin: 'The Sultan imagined it to be a defeat, but the events proved it to be warlike resolve' (وظنّها السلطان هزيمة وبانت بالعاقبة أنها كانت عزيمة). Baha', Schultens, 193--4 = Cairo, 173--4, states that Saladin had hoped to spin out the negotiations before Arsuf until the expected Turkmen reinforcements arrived, but the heat engendered by the dispute brought about an immediate move by the Crusaders, and Saladin was forced to draw up his forces for battle without delay.

the battle, and it would be difficult to substantiate Oman's argument that it 'gave the Franks the whole coast-land of Southern Palestine'.[1]

The Crusaders' halt at Jaffa put Saladin in a dilemma. Since he could not be certain whether they intended to march on Jerusalem, or whether his never-absent fears of a descent on Egypt were about to be realized, his first intention was to place a strong garrison in Ascalon to bar the way to Egypt. But on consulting his amirs, they argued that the Muslim forces were insufficient to garrison both Ascalon and Jerusalem, each of which would require twenty thousand fighting men, and bade him choose which of them he wished to hold and to destroy the defences of the other. Their argument was unanswerable, even if it was motivated in part by fear of another 'siege of 'Akka';[2] and sorrowfully, but resolutely, and realizing that there was no time to be lost, Saladin marched down to Ascalon and remained there until the work of dismantling was far advanced (12–24 September), while al-'Adil stood on guard outside Jaffa with a skeleton force. He then rode to Jerusalem to see to the strengthening of its defences, dismantled Ramlah and the castles in its vicinity, and on 1 October rejoined the main forces which had been posted at Ramlah in battle order.[3]

The complicated negotiations that now followed with Richard on the one hand and Conrad on the other were in a measure forces upon Saladin by the war-weariness of his troops, added to the difficulties of food, forage and equipment.[4] It seems

---

1. Charles Oman, *A History of War in the Middle Ages*, 2nd edn., London, 1924, vol. I, 318.
2. 'Imad, *Fath*, 389. Baha', Schultens, 198–9 = Cairo, 177–9, agrees in substance, but with less detail.
3. 'Imad, *Fath*, 390; Baha', Schultens, 202–3 = Cairo, 182–3.
4. 'Baha', Schultens, 200 = Cairo, 180, and especially the dispatches quoted in 'Imad, *Fath*, 392–3.

evident from the detailed accounts given by Baha' ad-Din that Saladin, though distrusting both, was more inclined to accept Conrad's proposals. 'If I were to die', he told Baha' ad-Din, 'it is most unlikely that these '*askars* would ever be brought together again, and the Franks would recover their strength. Our best policy is to continue to fight with them until we drive them out of Palestine.'[1] But Richard's offers found more favour with the commanders, for peace with him would mean the disbanding of the armies. Consequently, the report of the proposed marriage of Joan to al-'Adil (who would then take over the government of all Palestine) caused general rejoicing in the camp.[2] Richard's inconstancy, however, 'breaking every agreement as soon as it was made, and ever going back on his word',[3] wore out their patience, and ultimately Saladin had his way. His legate had actually been dispatched to Tyre to settle the terms of the alliance when Conrad was assassinated (28 April) to the general dismay of the Muslims.[4]

Meanwhile, the Crusaders had made their first advance to Bait Nuba, followed by their withdrawal to Ramlah and thence to rebuild Ascalon (21 January). Saladin's main efforts continued to be directed to the fortification of Jerusalem. The contingents from Mosul and Sinjar had returned to their homes, and were replaced on 22 December by an Egyptian contingent[5]; and he had in addition his Kurdish and Mamluk regiments (of whom the Asadiya were poised near Ascalon),[6] the troops of Damascus, and a force of Turkmen auxiliaries from Anatolia.[7]

---

1. Baha', Schultens, 218 = Cairo, 196–7.
2. 'Imad, *Fath*, 394.
3. 'Imad, *Fath*, 398.
4. Baha', Schultens, 239 = Cairo, 202; Cf. 'Imad, *Fath*, 422.
5. Ibn al-Athir, XII, 52; 'Imad, *Fath*, 399.
6. 'Imad, *Fath*, 418.
7. Baha', Schultens, 211 = Cairo, 190.

Avoiding any general engagement, therefore, Saladin's tactics were to use light forces, with Arab auxiliaries, to strike at their lines of communication, to hinder the movement of supplies, and to keep their main body occupied with skirmishes.

At the same time, he was harassed by further difficulties with his kinsmen. Taqi ad-Din's young son Nasir ad-Din Muhammad had, on his father's death, asked for confirmation of his father's fiefs, but Saladin, unwilling to entrust such wide powers to an inexperienced youth, imposed conditions. The young prince now revolted. Thereupon Saladin conferred the Mesopotamian provinces on his son al-Afdal, who left in February 1192 to refit his troops at Damascus, and prepared, with the assistance of his brother aZ-Zahir at Aleppo, to recover them from Nasir ad-Din. The latter in alarm appealed to al-'Adil to intercede for him, and eventually, after the negotiations with Richard in March and April, Saladin agreed to recall al-Afdal and made over the province to al-'Adil.[1]

The point on which these negotiations with the Crusaders foundered was Saladin's determination not to allow Ascalon to remain in the hands of the Crusaders.[2] Otherwise, an agreement was in sight, and towards the end of May, Saladin, expecting the arrival of the eastern contingents, allowed al-'Adil to leave the camp to take over his new possessions. It may have been due to the much diminished effectiveness with which Saladin was now operating that Richard suddenly resumed the offensive with the siege of Darum (23 May) and advanced towards Jerusalem early in June. Saladin again adopted the tactics of attcking his supply

---

1. One reason for the substitution may have been to ensure a firm control over the Zangids of Mosul. The arrangement was that Nasir ad-Din should, after one year, evacuate Mesopotamia and resume Taqi ad-Din's fief of Hamah and Ma'arra: 'Imad, *Fath*, 428. Al-'Adil was to retain at the same time his fiefs in Transjordan: Baha', Schultens, 277 = Cairo, 204.

2. 'Imad, *Fath*, 422.

lines, and with considerable success,[1] but was repaid in his own coin when Richard attacked and looted a caravan coming up from Egypt (23 June).[2]

In normal circumstances, the loss of a caravan would have passed as a natural risk of war. But when both sides were almost at breaking-point with strain and disappointment, such an incident might prove to be the crisis. The weight of the campaign was being borne by Saladin's personal troops, Kurds and mamluks, who had remained in the field almost without a break for four years. The caravan had been bringing them sorely needed supplies, animals and weapons, as well as reinforcements; the reinforcements were scattered, the supplies had gone to strengthen the enemy, and many no doubt had suffered much personal loss. For four years, the influence of Saladin's enthusiasm and the example of his resolution had kept up their morale, in face of continuous loss and retreat; but now, with nothing but the prospect of further loss, and even disaster, to crown the long, weary years of struggle, criticism and complaint, they were turning to mutiny. When Saladin took the resolve to destroy the wells and cisterns round Jerusalem and to prepare for a siege, and made his final appeal to the troops at the council on 1 July, it was the Kurd al-Mashtub who pledged their loyalty to him, while the mamluks were openly critical and insubordinate.[3]

To make matters worse, the contingents from Mosul, Sinjar and Diyar Bakr were already arrving at Damascus, but delaying

---

1. Baha', Schultens, 229, 230–1 = Cairo, 205–6, 207–8; 'Imad, *Fath*, 424; cf. *Itinerarium*, VI, c. 1. A fresh body of Turkmen arrived under Dilderim early in June, and the small contingent from Kafr Tab: Baha', Schultens, 229 = Cairo, 206.

2. Baha', Schultens, 231 sqq. = Cairo, 208 sqq., 'Imad, *Fath*, 425.

3. Baha', Schultens, 235–6 = Cairo, 212.

there.[1] The tension was relaxed, but not removed, by Richard's retreat and renewed proposals for a treaty, which as before broke on the issue of Ascalon, in spite of the eagerness of the troops for peace.[2] Once aroused, the spirit of mutiny and rivalry remained latent, and only needed an occasion to break out in sudden violence. The occasion came a few days later. Saladin, learning of Richard's intention to attack Beirut, sent al-Afdal to Marj 'Uyun with instructions to assemble there the eastern armies still at Damascus and to watch the situation.[3] He himself, with his personal troops, marched on Jaffa and in a furious three-day attack, forced a capitulation, exclusive of the citadel (31 July). This was too much for the troops, hot with desire to loot at last a captured town, and the Kurds and Turkmens burst in to gorge themselves with plunder.[4] The mamluks, however, stationed themselves at the gates of the town, and as the Kurds came out, seized heir loot from them and beat them up.[5]

This situation sufficiently explains the astonishing scenes that followed, when the indiscipline of the troops allowed the relief of the citadel of Jaffa by Richard; and again when, a few days later, Saladin attempted his *coup de main* on Richard's camp. In vain he ordered his troops to attack; squadron after squadron held back, and it was al-Mashtub's own brother who turned on him, saying 'Give your orders to those mamluks of yours who beat up the troops at Jaffa.'[6]

Thus Saladin's best and trustiest weapon had finally broken in his hands. But it had done its work; Richard's crusade was

---

1. 'Imad, *Fath*, 426, 428.
2. Baha', Schultens, 239–43 = Cairo, 215–19.
3. 'Imad, *Fath*, 428.
4. Baha', Schultens, 248 = Cairo, 222–4; 'Imad, *Fath*, 429.
5. Ibn al-Athir, XII, 55 (from *Barq*); the incident is referred to subsequently by Baha', Schultens, 254 = Cairo, 229–30, but not described at the time.
6. Baha', Schultens, 254 = Cairo, 229–30.

checkmated, and the eastern contingents came up in time to compel him to yield the point of Ascalon. Saladin, recovering from the humiliation before Jaffa, was eager to prosecute the struggle,[1] but was overborne by the remonstrances of the troops, and the armistice was duly signed on 2 September for a period of three years and eight months. Ironically enough, at this very moment, Saladin gained an unexpected accretion of power by the arrival of envoys, one from his old enemy, the powerful Shah-Arman of Khilat, offering his allegiance and the service of his troops, the other from the prince of Erzerum.[2] But the Crusade was over, and within a fortnight the armies were dispersed.

The Crusaders gained the coast from 'Akka to Jaffa, but not Ascalon, which remained unfortified. Saladin himself went to Jerusalem and then toured the castles and returned thence to Damascus. In February he greeted the pilgrims returning from the Hajj, and one evening was attacked by fever. All efforts were unable to check it, and on Wednesday, 4 March 1193, he died. One of those who knew him said, 'This was the only instance of a king's death that was truly mourned by the people.'[3]

---

1. 'Imad, *Fath*, 434–5; Baha', Schultens, 262 = Cairo, 236–7.
2. Baha', Schultens, 260 = Cairo, 235.
3. 'Abd al-Latif al-Baghdadi in Ibn Abi Usaybi'a, *'Uyun al-Anba'*, R.H.C., Or., III, 438.

Index

Note: Names with the prefix 'al-' are indexed under the capital letter immediately following. Subheadings are in chronological order.